INTERPRETATION
AND
TRANSFORMATION

Explorations in
Art and the Self

VIBS

Volume 187

Robert Ginsberg
Founding Editor

Peter A. Redpath
Exccutive Editor

Associate Editors

a volume in
Interpretation and Translation
IT
Michael Krausz, Editor

INTERPRETATION AND TRANSFORMATION

Explorations in Art and the Self

Michael Krausz

Amsterdam - New York, NY 2007

Cover Image: Michael Krausz, "Cipherspace," 2006

Cover Design: Studio Pollmann

The paper on which this book is printed meets the requirements of "ISO 9706:1994, Information and documentation - Paper for documents - Requirements for permanence".

ISBN-13: 978-90-420-2180-8
©Editions Rodopi B.V., Amsterdam - New York, NY 2007
Printed in the Netherlands

For Connie Costigan
~ again without whom ~

CONTENTS

Preface   xi

Acknowledgments   xiii

Introduction   1

Part One: Interpretation   5

ONE   Ideals of Interpretation   7

TWO   Singularism, Multiplism, and Their Differences   23

THREE   On the Idea of Multiplism   35

FOUR   Intentionality and its Objects   41

FIVE   On Imputation: Against Projectionism   49

SIX   Relativism and its Reference Frames   57

SEVEN   Constructive Realism: An Ontological Byway   71

Part Two: Transformation   83

EIGHT   Changing Reference Frames, Changing Emotions   85

NINE   Art and Self-Transformation: Creating and Becoming   97

TEN   Self-Transformation and Limits of Interpretation   103

Notes   123

Bibliography   133

About the Author   137

Index   139

How awry, altered and distorted everything and everyone was in these mirrors, how mockingly and unattainably did the face of truth hide itself behind all these reports, counter-reports and legends! What was still truth? What was still credible? And what would remain when I also learned about myself, about my own character and history from the knowledge in these archives?

Hermann Hesse
The Journey to the East

PREFACE

In the spirit of a philosophical psychologist, in the spring of 1992, I interviewed practitioners of Hindu and Buddhist soteriologies, or programs of self-realization. They included Swami Shyam Srivasta, of the Hindu Advaita Vedantic tradition, and the Dalai Lama, Tenzin Gyatso, of the Tibetan Mahayana Buddhist tradition. I asked Swami Shyam whether he and Mahayana Buddhists are talking about the same thing when addressing the ultimate nature of reality. He said yes, they are talking about the same thing, but the Buddhist is wrong. When I interviewed the Dalai Lama, I asked him whether the Mahayana Buddhist and the Advaita Vedantic Hindu are talking about the same thing. He said no, they are not talking about the same thing.

Here, I thought, was an intriguing dilemma: two persons were ostensibly disagreeing with each other about whether they are disagreeing with each other. To have a disagreement, contestants must be talking about the same thing. Without a common object of interpretation, contestants can neither agree nor disagree. This concept is applicable to a wide range of situations beyond the soteriologies I cite by way of example. Much of my philosophical work has focused on this issue since then.

The nature of disagreement gives rise to a series of interrelated philosophical questions under the rubric of the theory of interpretation. I previously addressed some of these questions in my *Rightness and Reasons* and *Limits of Rightness*.[1] For example, should we demand that any object of interpretation must answer to one and only one admissible interpretation? When should we count a series of artworks as one or more than one object of interpretation? When should we count a conjunction of interpretations as one or more than one interpretation? Further, what is the core aim of interpretation?

Since the publication of my earlier books, I have benefited from critical discussions, principally from those in Andreea Ritivoi's *Interpretation and its Objects: Studies in the Philosophy of Michael Krausz* and Michael McKenna's special issue of the journal *Philosophy in the Contemporary World* titled *Interpretation and Culture: Themes in the Philosophy of Michael Krausz*.[2] Those discussions have prompted me to elucidate and ramify key claims and to raise fresh issues.

In this work, I will ask further what bearing the aim of interpretation has on the range of ideally admissible interpretations. What is the relation between the aim of elucidation and edification? Is edification a legitimate aim of interpretive activity? What peculiarities about interpretive activity arise when we turn our attention to the interpretation of the interpreting self?

I affirm that elucidation is the core aim of interpretation. Yet, the aim of edification may enter into different relationships with the aim of elucidation. I argue that interpretations do not "project" properties on to an object of interpretation. Instead, objects of interpretation *have* properties—to be *found*—by virtue of the reference frames in which they are nested.

Further, I argue that the theory of interpretation is distinct but integrally related to the ontology of its objects. Interpretive activity is possible to the extent that its objects can be individuated and counted. I follow Bernard Harrison and Patricia Hanna in their suggestion that the identities of all objects are instantiated in the context of practices.

I claim that programs of self-transformation or self-realization seek both elucidatory and edificatory aims. But edificatory aims do not satisfy the core elucidatory aim of interpretation. Where the path toward self-realization involves the deconstruction of all dualisms—including that between subject and object—the requirement of the countability of objects of interpretation cannot be fulfilled. Since all interpretive activity presumes the distinction between subject and object, the aspired state of realization is beyond interpretation. Such is one limit of interpretation.

ACKNOWLEDGMENTS

While developing the ideas presented in this work, I have benefited from conversations with Leslie Anderson, Karen Bardsley, Noel Boulting, S. R. Bhatt, John Carvalho, David Cast, Vibha Chaturvedi, Cheryl Chen, Christoph Cox, David Crocker, Stephen Darwall, Robin Darwall-Smith, Rosemary Desjardins, Marcia Eaton, Catherine Elgin, Jeremy Elkins, Jay Garfield, Edward Grippe, Paul Grobstein, Chhanda Gupta, Lobsang Gyatso, Garry Hagberg, Patricia Hanna, Mark Harris, Bernard Harrison, Christine Koggel, Peter Lamarque, Nicholas Maxwell, Michael McKenna, Jitendranath Mohanty, Bo Mou, Nirmalangshu Mukherji, Giridhari Pandit, V. A. Rao, Andreea Ritivoi, Jill Stauffer, Paul Thom, Sam Wheeler, Anna Wierzbicka, Ellen Wright, and David Wong. Elizabeth D. Boepple provided invaluable editorial assistance. Lorraine Kirschner continues to provide professional support in too many ways to enumerate. With pleasure, I further acknowledge the formative roles played by extended conversations in the course of many years with Karl Popper, William Dray, Isaiah Berlin, José Ferrater-Mora, Joseph Margolis, Roman Jacobson, Tenzin Gyatso, and Shyam Srivasta—all of whom contributed in different ways to my development and understanding of themes related to this work.

Chapter six is reprinted with significant modifications from Michael Krausz, "Relativism and its Schemes," *Davidson's Philosophy and Chinese Philosophy: Philosophical Engagement*, ed. Bo Mou (Boston, Mass.: Brill Publishers, 2006, pp. 37–53). Materials for chapter eight have been drawn, with significant modifications, from Michael Krausz, "Changing One's Mind, Changing One's Emotions," *Philosophy from an Intercultural Perspective*, ed. Notker Schneider, Dieter Lohmar, Morteza Ghasepour, and Herman-Josef Scheidgen (Amsterdam and Atlanta: Rodopi, 1997), pp. 107–120. Materials for chapter nine, with significant modifications, were drawn from Michael Krausz, "Creating and Becoming," *The Concept of Creativity in Science and Art*, eds. Denis Dutton and Michael Krausz (The Hague: Martinus Nijhoff Publishers, 1981 and 1985), pp. 187–200.

INTRODUCTION

The concept of interpretation is open in the sense that it has no univocal and essentialist meaning, invariant among the myriad sorts of cases to which the term is characteristically applied.[1] So the best way to inquire into the nature of interpretation is to inspect representative cases to find patterns and tendencies among them without presuming some fixed prior criterion for their selection. Interpretation operates over such varied domains as the physical order, cultural entities, selves, religious experiences and more. We may learn about interpretation in one domain by comparing and contrasting it to interpretation in other domains. Nirmalangshu Mukherji observes:

> Much of what we grasp, understand, and act upon is a result of some interpretive activity directed on some object of interpretation. As Immanuel Kant taught us, little of the world comes to us via sensory channels only, so to speak. We interpret vagaries of nature, traffic signals, musical scores and performances, visual arts, speeches and writings, smiles and tears, gestures and attitudes, practices and symbols, aches and twinges, and so forth; each of these categories come in a bewildering variety of individual forms. Interpretive activities differ not only with respect to the objects, but with the features of interpreters as well—their age, gender, interests and preparations, cultural location, and the like. Discerning a general pattern in these activities is hard.[2]

The multifarious nature of interpretation as manifest in its diverse practices does allow for some general observations. Accordingly, in an effort to discern patterns of interpretive activity, I will freely draw upon a range of diverse examples. I will examine works of art such as Leonardo Da Vinci's *Last Supper,* Vincent Van Gogh's *The Potato Eaters,* Christo and Jean-Claude's *Gates,* Rembrandt van Rijn's *Self-Portraits,* Lucas Samaras' *Head Transformation*, and Chuck Close's *John*. Other examples include the length of a physical object, the River Ganges, a driver charged with speeding, the warmth of a hand, a dollar bill, and a point in a soccer game. Finally, I will include human emotions, the individual self and its realizations, the Hindu mantra "Thou Art That," the non-individual Supreme Self therein posited, and more. As well, I will recount some personal experiences.

Interpretation functions as both a noun and as a verb: as a product and as a process. Interpretation is both "productual" and "processual." While mindful of this symbiosis, I suggest that three features of interpretive activity persist. First, an interpretation is referential in the sense that it is *about* something distinct from itself. Second, interpretive activity involves judgments of salience or significance of features of designated objects of interpretation. Third, the core aim of interpretation is elucidation: it seeks broadly to "make sense" of, or to understand, pertinent objects of interpretation. In contrast, while elucidating an object of interpretation, an interpreter may seek to edify him or herself. Yet the aim of edification is distinct from the core aim of interpretation.

Like interpretation, the concept of transformation is open. For the purpose of this discussion, *transformation* concerns two dimensions: transformation of *objects* of interpretation in different handlings, how the object of interpretation gets transformed as pertinent activity proceeds; and transformation of interpreting *subjects*, how, in the course of interpretive activity, they may transform. Object-centered and subject-centered concerns are integrally related. Not only does a symbiotic relationship between these dimensions exist, but also, the very distinction between object and subject is presupposed in all interpretive activity. We cannot detach the understanding of interpretive activity from considerations concerning this and related dualisms, the application of which depends upon personal programs or projects of transformation. Some such programs are hospitable to interpretive activity. Others are not.

More fully, I hold that the core aim of interpretation is to make sense of, or to *elucidate*, its objects. The *Oxford English Dictionary* defines elucidation and its cognates in terms of rendering something clear or intelligible. I understand it generally to include explaining or making sense. Yet a person might pursue other aims or goals—even simultaneously—such as edification or transformation. The *Oxford English Dictionary* defines edification in terms of a process tending toward moral or spiritual improvement. I understand it more generally to include self-cultivation, healing, liberation, or emancipation, including self-realization or self-transformation.

Paul Thom offers a version of the difference between elucidation and edification in his distinction between understanding and consolation. He says:

> Consolation requires not knowledge but hope. A consoling message is not so much one we know that is true, as one we hope will be fulfilled. We must believe fulfillment of the message to be possible. But belief in a possibility is a far cry from knowledge. The consolations offered by the great religions often concern matters about which no knowledge is possible, one way or the other. Precisely because we cannot know that their claims are false, we can cling to the hope that they may be realized.[3]

So understood, the aim of edification is not so much to explain or understand a phenomenon as to help alleviate suffering or to promote human flourishing.

For two interpretations to compete, they must not only address the same things, they must also pursue the same aim. Call this the "same-aims-proviso." Accordingly, consider Thom's example of interpreting the phenomenon of death:

What does an interpretation of the fact of death aim at? Does it aim at understanding, or consolation? Those who have knowledge about the causes of death, about the phases in the process, about the phenomenology of death, and so forth might achieve an understanding of death. We may not find such knowledge consoling as we approach our death.

An attempt to provide consolation might come into conflict with an attempt to provide understanding, if for example it offered consolation on the basis of some proposition that can be known to be false. The consolation will be ineffective as soon as its recipient discovers that it is based on a falsehood. Such would-be consolers should ensure that they offer their wares only to the ignorant.

But, so long as the recipient does not know that the basis of the consolation is false—even better, if that basis cannot be known to be false, because it is unfalsifiable—then no conflict occurs between consolation and understanding. I can know all to be known about death, and still take consolation from an interpretation that offers me hope, so long as that consolation is not based on falsifiable propositions. If knowledge offers me no hope, I derive hope from elsewhere.[4]

Accordingly, a message that aims to give hope (edification) is one which aims toward something other than elucidation. To be sure, as Thom says, if the message is known to be false, it will be ineffective when taken to edify.

Edification is characteristically associated with elucidation. Individuals typically impart a personal narrative, however sketchy, about where they have been and, by implication, where they wish to go. In the psychotherapeutic case, a personal narrative may include elucidating functions or dysfunctions that motivate change. In the Vedantic case, the elucidation of suffering and its causes will help to motivate an individual's soteriological changes. In another case, a person might seek to adopt a program of edification without elucidation, presuming that *any* elucidatory activity inhibits edification. To be sure, elucidation can sometimes inhibit edification. But edification without elucidation lacks direction. In still another case, a person who pursues elucidation might profess to be entirely disinterested in edification. But might they only be failing to recognize edificatory effects of elucidatory effort?

Finally, a person may aim for neither elucidation nor edification. Such a posture might arise from an attitude of indifference, or it may reflect the satisfaction of a state of realization already achieved. These possibilities may obtain in stages—where a person may pursue edification with or without elucidation, or elucidation with or without edification. Insofar as the core aim of interpretive activity is elucidation, interpretive activity may or may not, at any given stage, be involved with edification. Interpretive activity may, but need not, lead to edification.

Edification is not a core aim of interpretation. Yet persons' edificatory practices may depend upon some interpreted presuppositions. While their practices are typically *associated with* interpreting, edifying is not interpreting. For example, taking communion may edify by providing meaning and structure to a life, without regard to the "truth" or "admissibility" of utterances spoken on such occasions, even if, on other occasions, they may be taken as assertions to be evaluated accordingly. Similarly, the practice of keeping kosher may edify in that it may provide a sense of a shared history and community without regard to the truth or elucidatory status of its presuppositions.

Thom is right to say that we cannot effectively pursue an edificatory program whose presuppositions we have judged to be false. At the same time, the very activity of elucidating—the choice of examples, the aspects featured, the judgments of adequacy of interpretations advanced, and the rest—are affected by persons' programs or projects of edification. Interpreters' views of what is good for their flourishing or realization affect the way in which they conduct elucidatory inquiry. In this way, the aims of elucidation and edification are in symbiosis. So seen, interpretive activity involves an interaction between different sorts of aims, one of which should be countenanced as the core aim of interpretation.

Part One

INTERPRETATION

One

IDEALS OF INTERPRETATION

1. Singularism and Multiplism

Consider some central distinctions and strategies that fall under the elucidatory aims of interpretive activity. In *Rightness and Reasons* and *Limits of Rightness*, I offered definitions of singularism and multiplism based on the distinction between interpretations and objects of interpretation.[1] In those works, I divided theorists of interpretation into two groups. *Singularists* assume every object of interpretation answers to only one single ideally admissible interpretation. In contrast, *multiplists* assume that some objects of interpretation can have more than one ideally admissible incongruent interpretation. Further, in a given case, a singularist condition would be fulfilled if a one-to-one relation between an interpretation and its object of interpretation existed. A multiplist condition would be fulfilled if a many-to-one relation between interpretations and their common object of interpretation existed. Also, we may have good reasons for preferring one of several admissible interpretations without resulting in a singularist condition.

Notice that singular*ism* and multipl*ism* are *asymmetrical* in the sense that singularism mandates a single admissible interpretation for *any* object of interpretation. In contrast, multiplism allows that in *some* cases multiplist conditions obtain.

The application of these ideals is not a straightforward matter. Sometimes, the object of interpretation is a single thing, for instance, a single painting. At other times, the object of interpretation is a collection of single things, such as a group of paintings. Whether—in both of these cases—the object of interpretation should be taken as a single thing, is an open question.

Different commentators have variously interpreted *The Potato Eaters* as formalist, Marxist, feminist, or psychological in nature. The formalist interpretation addresses such formal features as the vertical, horizontal, and oblique lines of the painting, along with such formal parallels as those between the closely placed mugs on the table and the unity of the depicted family. The Marxist-feminist interpretation addresses the painting's depiction of manual labor and features the historical context in which Vincent Van Gogh produced it. The psychological interpretation concentrates on the expressiveness of depicted characters in relation to the inner conflicts in Van Gogh's life. For example, some psychological interpretations emphasize that the figures in the painting do not look directly at each other. They appear lonely and isolated. The two men are turned toward the elderly woman to the viewer's right, but she looks downward. We can take this and other features of the painting as a basis on which to speak of Vincent's longing for kindness and the like.[2]

In his early adult career, Anselm Kiefer concerned himself with monumental images (such as *Shulamith*, 1983) reminiscent of sites associated with Germany's Nazi past. He depicted cavernous spaces evoking crematoria or railway tracks leading to death camps. He also created more general visual testimonials to German history and culture. As well, his photographs feature himself at significant Nazi sites. They show him giving Hitler's "Sieg Heil" salute. Kiefer's collection of single paintings have been multiply interpreted. They have prompted some people to interpret his works as *celebrating* the memories of that terrible time, charging him with being a neo-Nazi. Others see the matter differently. They offer an *exorcist* interpretation, according to which they understand Kiefer as having engaged in a kind of cathartic effort for himself and for his generation of post-war Germans. They view him to have vicariously relived Nazi history in order to overcome it, to purge it—like a patient who relives a trauma in order to exorcise it.[3]

I take these sets of interpretations of Van Gogh's single paintings and Kiefer's collection of paintings respectively to exemplify *multiple interpretability*. In each case, the interpretations are incongruous. Yet they are jointly admissible.

These cases allow us to distinguish between the singularist and multiplist conditions in terms of a two-term scheme, between interpretation(s) and their objects of interpretation. The singularist condition obtains where a one-to-one relation between interpretation and its object of interpretation exists. The multiplist condition obtains where a many-to-one relation between interpretations and their object of interpretation obtains.

2. Interpretive Projects

Ernst Van De Wetering offers a sketch of the current state of interpretations of Rembrandt van Rijn's *Self-Portraits*. He says that the collection is sometimes interpreted as revelatory of Rembrandt's process of *Identity-Formation,* and other times they are interpreted as *Commodities.* The Identity-Formation interpretation is:

> the long held and still prevalent view that Rembrandt created his sequence of self-portraits as private works and that in these works he was primarily preoccupied with aspects of his own identity . . . [H. P. Chapman says] "Rembrandt's self-portraits have the qualities of personal works, generated by internal pressures. His lifetime preoccupation with self-portraiture can be seen as a necessary process of identity formation or self-definition."[4]

Accordingly, some interpreters viewed Rembrandt as someone (quoting Chapman again) "with 'heightened self-consciousness' and 'a unique drive to self-explorations,' [who] created 'product(s) of penetrating self-scrutiny.'"[5] At the same time, the Identity-Formation interpretation contrasts with the *Commodity* interpretation. Van De Wetering cites Eddy de Jongh as embracing the Commodity interpretation. He says:

> While Chapman saw Rembrandt's self-portraits as works created on his own initiative, documenting self-interest and self-fashioning, De Jongh presumed that in Rembrandt's time a self-portrait, including one by Rembrandt, was seen *in the first place* as a commodity. Self-portraits, according to De Jongh, were collector's items for a small elite. He compares them to portraits of philosophers or other distinguished figures which were also collector's items at the time.[6]

While Van De Wetering suggests that the Identity Formation and the Commodity interpretations are opposed (if not contradictory), Susan Fegley Osmond suggests that the two interpretations may co-exist side by side. She writes:

> In his early years, he [Rembrandt] likely knew that using himself as a model for tronies would help his face become a household item and increase his reputation. As time went on, while a ready market remained for his self-portrayals, his internal motivation may have altered or at least broadened. At times, he used the self-portrait as a forum to broadcast a persona. At others, in showing himself playing a role such as the prodigal son, a potentate, or an artist of the past, he could by allusion make comments about aspects of his inner state or his status in the flow of history. In most of the late works, contemplation of himself as an individual and as a representative of humanity seems to have played a major part.[7]

A point of logic arises here. Osmond assumes that the Identity Formation and the Commodity interpretations may be pursued side by side, that they may be conjoined without incongruence. I suggest that these jointly admissible interpretations are incongruent and they actually provide a fruitful way to articulate what kind of condition incongruence is. The Identity Formation and Commodity interpretations are not contradictory. They are conjoined without formal contradiction. Yet they are functionally opposed. Each competes with the other as a contestant for being embraced "in the first place" as Van De Wetering puts it.

The two interpretations are *incongruent* in the sense that they are products of interpreters' opposed *interpretive projects*. Accordingly, an object of interpretation is logically secondary to, and parasitic upon, an interpretive project. When considering Rembrandt's self-portraits, for example, our interests and purposes motivate a choice of project and reference frame, which then may determine the number of objects of interpretation. What is suggestive about the Rembrandt example is that the projects, which claim our attention in the first place, are contentious. Van Der Wetering criticizes the Identity Formation interpretation by suggesting that the Identity-Formation hypothesis is anachronistic, for, as he quotes Charles Taylor, "Talk about 'identity' in the modern sense would have been incomprehensible to our forebears of a couple of centuries ago."[8] Van De Wetering quotes Taylor further saying, "we have to remind ourselves that the full question of identity belongs to the post-Romantic period which is marked by the idea . . . that each person has his or her own way of being."[9]

I suggest that we should understand the tension between the Identity Formation and the Commodity interpretations in terms of the competing interpretive projects—pre- or post-romantic—that motivate each of them. Depending upon from which project one speaks, one or the other interpretation will assume the "first place" of attention, but it does not thereby assume logical priority.

Directed against the Identity Formation interpretation, the charge of anachronism may be a good reason for *preferring* the Commodity interpretation, but not a sufficiently strong reason to eliminate the Identity Formation interpretation as inadmissible. Because the pertinent interpretation is anachronistic is an inconclusive ground for disallowing it. Yet anachronism is a reason for not preferring it. For a Marxist historian of art, for example, anachronism is a weak ground for disallowance. So to ask, "What are Rembrandt's works *really*—Identity Formative or Commodity?" as if only one of these will do, makes no sense. No contradiction exists in saying that the self-portraits answer to both interpretations. Yet those interpretations are opposed in the sense that each arises from different interpretive projects.

The Rembrandt example also shows how the interpretive project affects the way objects of interpretations should be counted, how their numbers should be calculated. Consider Van De Wetering's remarks:

The usual reaction to the large number of self-portraits that Rembrandt produced is one of surprise; yet when the numbers usually cited are added up (c. 30 etchings, c. 40 paintings and some seven drawings) this is in effect only to count every occasion on which Rembrandt sat down before the mirror in order to depict his own face. To regard solely these works as the self-portraits is to see them in the first place from the point of view of the artist; but if, on the other hand, one regards Rembrandt's self-portraits as commodities, one arrives at a different calculation.

Even if one limits oneself to those works that one can consider as proper 'portraits' of Rembrandt (viz., excluding tronies, studies etc.) there must have been hundreds. Not only the copies after Rembrandt's painted self-portraits and the painted workshop variants . . ., but also every single impression of the etchings bearing Rembrandt's likeness, must often have been considered as (self-) portraits of Rembrandt.[10]

In forthcoming chapters, I will pursue the role of interpretive projects and reference frames in interpretive activity. For the remainder of this chapter, let us keep in mind the Van Gogh, Kiefer, and Rembrandt examples as I rehearse conceptual and strategic issues in relation to singularism and multiplism.

3. Singularism and Multiplism: Conceptual and Strategic Issues

Here is how David Novitz states his singularist position:

> It is always possible to show of two apparently competing interpretations either that they do not really compete, or that if they do, both are false, or that the one is true, and other false. Where interpretation is concerned, I argue, bivalence rules; there is and can be only one true interpretation.[11]

In turn, Joseph Margolis formulates his multiplism in this way:

> Claims and judgments that on a bivalent logic would be or would yield incompatibles can be shown to be (formally) consistent by suitably replacing or supplementing bivalence, in context, with a many valued logic.[12]

As a point of terminology, I distinguish between singular*ism* and multipl*ism* on the one hand, and singular*ist* and multipl*ist* *conditions* on the other hand. The first set of terms contrast generalized ideals. Singularism mandates that *every* object of interpretation answers to one and only one ideally admissible interpretation. Multiplism mandates that *some* objects of interpretation answer to more than one ideally admissible interpretation. So stated, singularism and multiplism are mutually exclusive and jointly contradictory. In contrast, a second set of terms—singularist *conditions* versus multiplist *conditions*—does not address generalized ideals but particular cases. A particular case can answer to a "singularist condition" or to a "multiplist condition" but not both, if *it* does or does not answer to one or more ideally admissible interpretations. This difference in terms will prove to be key when we consider Bernard Harrison and Patricia Hanna's suggestion that a *given* object of interpretation may answer *both* to a singularist and a multiplist condition.

For the multiplist, the reasonableness of one interpretation does not disallow the reasonableness of an alternative interpretation. That does not mean, though, that any interpretation will do. The interpretive tolerance afforded by the multiplist is no invitation to anarchy. For while more than one interpretation may be admissible, other interpretations are inadmissible. The multiplist is just as concerned as the singularist is to jettison inadmissible interpretations. Yet the multiplist holds that some interpretations exist that are inadmissible and for pertinent cases more than one interpretation is admissible. Further, multiplism affirms that any progress made toward converging upon a limited range of admissible interpretations does not entail a progress toward a single admissible interpretation. Narrowing the range of admissible interpretations entails no singularist condition. A multiplist condition is taken not to arise from an epistemic lack.

Notice that the elimination of false interpretations is compatible with a singularist *and* a multiplist approach. Both the singularist and the multiplist seek to eliminate inadmissible interpretations. But the elimination of inadmissible interpretations does not mandate that there *must be* one true interpretation or that we should gear our inquiry as if there were such an interpretation. Further, insofar as we are concerned with the issue of admissibility—whether along singularist or multiplist lines—its object of interpretation must be countable. Countability of objects of interpretation is a necessary condition of interpretation.

4. Let a Thousand Flowers Bloom

Both singularists and multiplists can embrace the thought that we should encourage as many contestants as possible. Singularist David Crocker says:

> Let a thousand flowers bloom, not because (after weeding) each bloom is justified, but because the evaluation of the diversity will contribute to achievement of the one prize bloom.[13]

Yet a multiplist can as well embrace the thought that we should let "a thousand" candidates be considered. But, "in the end," there may be more than one "winner." To say that, in the end, more than one winner will emerge, is not to say that just any flower will qualify as a winner. After all, some flowers are weeds.

We might worry that we have an infinite number of flowers with which to deal. But such a worry is needless. At any state of inquiry, a finite number of flowers to consider exists. We should understand admissibility within the context of a finite number of contestants, even though there might always emerge yet other contestants. Though an indefinitely large number of contestants may exist in principle, it does not follow that we cannot proceed on the assumption that, for any given contest, we may still have a range of ideally admissible winners. Because a finite number of winners might exist does not mandate that that number should be either one or more than one.

We could hold that multiplism is conducive to tolerance and the understanding of others. But multiplism is no requisite for tolerance and understanding. A singularist could be as tolerant and understanding as a multiplist could be. A singularist might actively encourage the formulation and pursuit of many alternative interpretations—not as finally admissible but because they might be suggestive in the very pursuit of a single admissible interpretation. We could see such an active encouragement as healthy for critical discourse in general. So we should not uniquely tie intolerance or oppression to singularism and tolerance or understanding to multiplism.

5. Incongruence

The tension between singularists and multiplists is reflected in their respective tolerances for interpretations that are incongruent but not jointly contradictory. Singularists think of incongruence in bivalent terms, according to which any second interpretation opposed to a first interpretation is taken to be contradictory to it, and so all but one interpretation should be rejected as inadmissible. The multiplist, on the other hand, holds that we need not understand incongruence in such bivalent terms. Multiplists allow that incongruence or tension may exist between contending interpretations, a tension with opposition but without exclusivity. While singularists deploy the bivalent values of truth and falsity, multiplists deploy such multivalent values as reasonableness, appropriateness, or aptness, and they allow that more than one interpretation may be admissible. Multiplists allow that incongruent interpretations may be jointly defended, *but disallow their being conjoined as one.*

Margolis says that two interpretations are incongruent when—*if they were in a bivalent logic*—they would be contradictory. But in a multivalent logic they are not contradictory. More fully, he says:

> When . . . I say that "we allow seemingly incompatible accounts of a given work . . . to stand as confirmed," I mean to draw attention to the fact that the accounts in question would be incompatible construed in terms of a model of truth and falsity, but are *not* incompatible construed in terms of plausibility. We have, then, succeeded in showing the coherence of a critical practice that tolerates the joint defensibility of interpretive judgments that, on a model of truth and falsity, would be incompatible.[14]

Here is another formulation of Margolis' "robust relativism."

> It posits the . . . thesis that we may introduce by fiat any consistent logical constraints we care to admit on the truth-values or truth-like values particular sets of claims or claims in particular sectors of inquiry may take. We may, by fiat alone, deny to a given sector the power of pertinent claims or judgments to take bipolar truth-values . . .; and then, by introducing logically weaker values, we may admit claims or judgments to be evidentially supported or supportable even where, on a bipolar model of truth-values but not now, admissible judgments would yield incompatible or contradictory claims. We may, abandon excluded middle or *tertium non datur*. On the new model such judgments could be said to be "incongruent."[15]

Margolis' suggestion for a multi-valued account of incongruence is an important step in formulating the multiplist program. Yet here is a problem with Margolis' approach. The replacement of bivalent logic by multivalent logic does immunize a would-be contradiction. But as his formulation stands, that immunization appears to be too strong. For it might render the conjunction of incongruent interpretations with no strains at all. Without some strain, there would be no reason to count incongruent interpretations as incongruent. We might see them as being seamlessly conjoinable. But they are not.

6. Incongruence: A Supplement

I offer a supplementing account of incongruence meant to disallow the conjoining of two incongruent admissible interpretations into a single admissible interpretation. My account preserves the necessary strain between the two incongruent admissible interpretations so as not to allow their being seamlessly conjoinable.

The *Oxford English Dictionary* defines the term, "congruous," in terms of the theory of numbers: "If the difference between A and B be divisible by number P, A is said to be congruous to B *for the modulus* P."[16] So understood, congruence is not a two-term relation between A and B, but a *three-term relation*. A and B are congruent *in relation to a modulus P.*[17] Put otherwise, A and B are congruent by virtue of a common modulus. As examples, Eric Weisstein speaks of the moduli of hours and twelve-hour clocks. He says:

> Since there are 60 minutes in an hour, "minute arithmetic" uses a modulus of m = 60. If one starts at 40 minutes past the hour and then waits another 35 minutes, 40 + 35 = 15 ([where the modulus is] mod 60), so the current time would be 15 minutes past the (next) hour. Similarly, "hour arithmetic" on a 12-hour clock uses a modulus of m = 12, so 10 o'clock (a.m.) plus five hours gives 10 + 5 = 3 (mod 12), or 3 o'clock (p.m.)[18]

Or, to use another example of Weisstein's: "When computing the time of day using a 12-hour clock obtained by adding four hours to 9:00, the answer [is] 1:00." Here the modulus is 12. If we use the civilian modulus of a 12-hour clock, 12 hours plus 1 hours equals 1 p.m. In turn, if one uses the military modulus of 24 hours, 24 hours plus 1 hour equals 1 a.m.

The modulus is a *reference frame*, as I more generally refer to it, in relation to which the calculation is made. It allows for degrees of formality or informality, as in the cases of the clocks or Rembrandt's self-portraits. Notice that the idea of congruence here embraced is a three-term condition. Where two interpretations are congruous, they are so in relation to a third thing, a reference frame. Further, in the examples considered (civilian and military clocks), the reference frames are inter-translatable without residue. Where they are not so intertranslatable, we may say that they are incongruent. Keep in mind, too, that the adoption of a reference frame is a matter of convention in accord with one's interests and purposes. Reasons can be given for adopting one or the other. Yet once adopted—in cases like the clocks—only one correct answer about the time exists.

The contrast case of congruence is not straightforward. For where no common reference frame exists, it does not follow that (as we might otherwise expect) the result is one of incongruence. Absence of a common reference frame may result in either incongruence or non-congruence, where the non-congruence is understood to be a condition in which the two interpretations are irrelevant to one another, where no pertinent tension obtains between the interpretations in question. The reference frame of a military clock is, in this sense, non-congruent with, say, an irrelevant geocentric or heliocentric model of the solar system. In short, for two interpretations to be incongruent, beyond the absence of a common reference frame, a pertinent condition of relevance must be in place.

7. On Counting Objects of Interpretation and Their Interpretations

Counting an object of interpretation as one or more, or counting an interpretation as one or more is no straightforward matter. In order to install a singularist condition we might *"pluralize"* an object of interpretation that first might appear to answer to two opposing interpretations. In so doing, we might install a one-to-one relation between the pluralized objects of interpretation and distinct interpretations. Or, to install the singularist condition, we might seek to "aggregate" pertinent interpretations into one. In that way, a one-to-one relation between object of interpretation and interpretation would also be installed. Conversely, in order to install a multiplist condition, we may pluralize interpretations, separating them into distinct interpretations. In this way, a many-to-one relation between interpretations and object of interpretation may be installed. Or, we may aggregate different objects of interpretation, and affirm that the aggregated result answers to more than one interpretation.

For example, in the case of musical interpretation, singularist Nicholas Maxwell pluralizes objects of interpretation to install a singularist condition. He pluralizes works of music. He holds that interpreters of music create new works. He says:

> The performer re-creates—or co-creates—the work of art . . . What we have, in short, in the case of the performing arts, is not one work of art and many different equally correct adjunct interpretations, but many different works of art, all sharing common features, and stemming from a common source, a common set of instructions.[19]

According to him, only one interpretation for any given musical work is admissible, because the result of co-creation is "hydra-headed." Accordingly, conductor Riccardo Muti, say, cannot interpret the same work on two different occasions. Instead, on different occasions, he must interpret different works.

Here is another example of how, by pluralizing the object of interpretation, a singularist might seek to deconstruct what initially appears to be a multiplist condition. The Ganges River runs through the Indian city of Varanasi where the holy are wrapped and "buried" in the river's bottom by being sunken with attached rocks. The "holy" include Hindu Saddhus, Buddhist monks, and babies. The Ganges is also a river in which the ashes of cremated bodies of the unholy are disposed; a river in which people pray and meditate; and a river on which boats traverse, both by oars and by motor. In this river, people brush their teeth, wash themselves, and do laundry. In the Ganges, people dispose of buffalo carcasses. People use the Ganges in all these ways.

Some Varanasians distinguish between the *inside* of the Ganges and the *outside* of the Ganges. They see the outside of the Ganges as a germ-infested dumpsite, and the inside as morally and metaphysically pure. Someone who seeks to install a singularist condition might pluralize the object of interpretation in this way—by designating that the pure and holy Ganges is its "inner" nature, and that the dumpsite is its "outer" nature. By referring to the holy and the non-holy Ganges, we could argue that we are referring to different Rivers Ganges. By doing so, we might seek to dissolve any incongruence between the "holy site" interpretation and the "dumpsite" interpretation. We would be addressing different things.

Here is a case in which the numeral identity of an object of interpretation is essentially contestable. In February 2005, Christo and Jeanne-Claude installed *The Gates* in New York City's Central Park. What was it? How many things were *The Gates*? When people spoke of it, what were they talking about? When they apparently disagreed with each other, were they talking about the same thing? Were they disagreeing about what they *should* be talking about? Were they involved in different interpretive projects?

Consider a sample of interpretations of *The Gates*. Edward Sozanski, for example, asks, "What exactly, is the Gates?" He answers:

> The Central Park extravaganza called The Gates by the artists Christo and Jeanne-Claude turned out to be a spectacular people magnet. . . . Give the artists credit for creating a spectacular public event . . . as art, the big-footed, 16-foot-tall "gates"—gallowslike frames hung with pleated fabric panels that arched over 23 miles of park walkways— defined banality. . . . The Gates might have been a marvel of logistic deployment, but even at first glance one could see that it had little to offer besides its massive scale, which struck me primarily as an expression of artistic ego. The frames, 16 feet tall and clad in garish orange plastic, were as ugly as gargoyles and not nearly as charming. . . . The nylon curtains that hung down to within seven feet of the ground were dispro-

portionately small; as a colleague observed, they looked like kitchen curtains flapping in the breeze. (And cheap ones at that.) . . . through some mysterious process not wholly attributable to promotion and advertising, it became not just a major public event but a communal ritual. . . . Its transience . . . and its once-in-a-lifetime quality undoubtedly contributed to the mild mass hysteria. Like a local team in the Super Bowl or the World Series, it was something that people had to experience so it could be talked about later.[20]

The Gates appear to be, at minimum, two sorts of things: (1) frames with fabric panels, and (2) a public event or communal ritual. Which is it? Well, the answer depends upon the interpreter's reference frame in which interpretations of "it" would be nested. Qua frames hung with fabric panels, for Sozanski, *The Gates* is unsatisfactory. Qua public event, "it was something that people had to experience." We find the same dichotomy between these quas in other interpretations. Miriam Hill emphasizes that *The Gates* is a special event when she writes:

It was a happening—people talked as if they were at Woodstock. . . . Thora Jacobson, director of Philadelphia's Samuel S. Fleisher Art Memorial, joined a group of Philadelphians for a tour. She loved The Gates, and the controversy. . . ." It stirs debate," she said . . . they're redefining what art is in a lot of ways, so that in and of itself is valuable to me."[21]

Peter Schjeldahl says:

how people behave during the installation is what it is for and about . . . Those who deplore "The Gates" as ugly aren't wrong, just poor sports . . . The nylon fabric is sullen to the touch. The proportions of the arches are graceless, and dogs alone esteem the clunky bases. [Yet] it will be [something] pitiable to have missed.[22]

Mark Stevens says:

[The Gates] . . . as event, as spectacle, as public gesture—whoah." . . . Christo and Jeanne-Claude's *The Gates* is a spectacle . . . a piece of elaborate social theatre that's an unintentional portrait of our time. . . . The color of the translucent fabric hanging from the gates isn't quite right, at least for my eye, despite the ever-changing effects of light . . . it looks more like a Wal-Mart orange that cuts too harshly across the subtle winter landscape. . . . *The Gates* also lacks the formal concentration that a great artist brings to painting or sculpture. But its whoah—well, there's no denying the pleasurable hit. . . . As an American extravaganza, *The Gates* is much more interesting than, say, the halftime show at the Super Bowl. . . . The Woodstock air that filled the park on the week-end *The Gates* opened, when strangers talked to one another and pilgrims from outside New York came to admire the spectacle, was enjoyable to everyone but professional grouches and, predictably, the art world.[23]

By distinguishing between (1) supporting frames with fabric panels, and (2) a public event, do two interpretations of the "same thing" confront us? Or, are we confronted with two things, each answering to different interpretations? Qua frames, "the work" fails according to the critics cited. Qua event, some interpreters believe *The Gates* to be a spectacular success. Do these verdicts oppose one another? They do not if we keep the quas distinct, if we keep distinct the reference frames through which they are seen. They do not oppose each other if we pluralize the object of interpretation. Yet whether we aggregate or pluralize the frames and the event—whether we bring them together as one or separate them as two—is a matter of particular interests and purposes.

How is it that the choice of reference frames may be warranted in relation to designated interests and purposes? Motivated by pertinent projects, qua dog-walker, we will see the frames' posts as potential stations; qua fabric maker, we will see the panels as material; qua establishment subversive, we will see the installation as a commentary on the aestheticist tradition of precious objects. The insistence that seeing things in different ways is only an epistemic matter clouds the thought that no one thing exists there prior to reference frames with features or facets waiting to be seen through reference frames. We must take seriously the thought that what exists there, is so, by virtue of its place in a reference frame and not independently of such placement.

8. Perpetual Pluralism

Notice that, as in Maxwell's handling of the musical case, a person who *perpetually* pluralizes the object of interpretation in order to avoid a multiplist condition would avoid any conflict between any interpretations. For any interpretation, a unique object of interpretation would be postulated. But—apart from a question-begging commitment to universal singularism—we have no reason why the pluralizing of objects of interpretation should be involved in all cases. Instead, we need to judge the appropriateness of deploying the pluralizing or aggregating strategies in a piecemeal way.

We can turn the worry about the perpetual pluralizer of objects of interpretations on its head. We could as well worry about the multiplist who, in the face of a multiplicity of interpretations, perpetually aggregates objects of interpretation in order that *any* would-be singularist case would be cast into a multiplist case. We might do so by perpetually aggregating objects of interpretation initially considered to be more than one. In the extreme, all objects would be "hyphenated" into one and were we to offer incongruent admissible interpretations of it, a super-multiplist condition would obtain.

Perpetual aggregating appears to be the tendency of those who speak of "the World" or "all that is" as their object of interpretation. A singularist might insist that for such a hyphenated object of interpretation, one grand, single admissible interpretation of it exists.

9. On Not Combining Incongruent Interpretations

Here is an argument against conjoining two sets of incongruent interpretations. As indicated, an interpretation is warranted if it accounts for the salient or significant features of an object of interpretation. Yet sets of incongruent interpretations are not conjoinable into a single "comprehensive" interpretation, because otherwise the properties initially taken as salient—or "italicized"—would be undone. Doing so displaces, instead of enhances, the saliences taken separately. When conjoined, the initial italics is displaced. When two sets of incongruent salient features are conjoined, the conjunction does not result in the simple addition of the two. Each displaces the other as initially weighted. If we first italicize designated features, and then later we italicize other features around it, the original italics do not retain their original force. The conjunction alters the relative weight of the sets of italics when taken separately. I call this phenomenon the *condition of displaced italics*. As Peter Lamarque says, "Too many saliences jostling for attention blur rather than enhance [otherwise separated interpretations]."[24]

In sum, singularism should not be guaranteed by *perpetually* pluralizing objects of interpretation or by *perpetually* aggregating interpretations. Multiplism should not be guaranteed by *perpetually* aggregating objects of interpretation or by *perpetually* pluralizing interpretations. We should judge the applicability of these strategies in a piecemeal way, depending upon pertinent interests and purposes.

10. Interaction between Interpretations: Da Vinci's *Last Supper*

While multiplists characteristically tolerate incongruence *between* admissible interpretations—taking such incongruence as a basis for distinguishing between them—singularist Maxwell tolerates incongruence *within* a single admissible interpretation. He supports his view by adducing examples of interpretations of Leonardo Da Vinci's *Last Supper*, especially that of Leo Steinberg in contrast with that of Johann Wolfgang von Goethe.[25] In summary, art historian Michael Podro tells us that according to Goethe's interpretation, the subject of the painting, taken as a single represented moment, "is the consternation of the disciples at Christ foretelling his betrayal."[26]

As a product of Enlightenment thought, Podro takes *Last Supper* to lack theological dimension. He also suggests that, according to Steinberg, the painting, taken as representing *two* moments, is about betrayal *and* about the institution of the sacrament of the Eucharist. For Steinberg, the painting is pluralized, from one to two moments, and each answers to different distinct singularist conditions (only one lacking in theological dimension). But according to Podro, that is only a first step because Steinberg introduces a higher order comprehensive interpretation. Steinberg's argument "is not that the announcement of betrayal is absent from the painting, but that it is *absorbed* in this greater meaning."[27] So understood, what first appears as two distinct admissible interpretations of a given object of interpretation, becomes—in Steinberg's handling—a single hyphenated interpretation. Where the larger interpretation is counted as one, an internal incongruence exists. Steinberg's incorporation resists the use of incongruence as a criterion for individuating between interpretations.

Andrew Butterfield emphasizes Steinberg's penchant for embracing "contradictory possibilities" within a given interpretation. (Notice that Butterfield fails to distinguish between contradiction, contrariness, and incompatibility.) Butterfield says:

> Steinberg attacks the standard view of the painting as a modern and secular invention. He claims the "the impoverishment of its content down to pure psychodrama is our legacy from the Age of Enlightenment. . . . The modern interpretation of *Cenacolo* begins with the repudiation of its sacramental component." . . . Steinberg believes instead that nearly every feature of the painting suggests multiple and contradictory possibilities. Others wanted to see it as an illustration of one moment of the narrative, while he sees it as depicting two. In a similar manner, he says that the gestures, space, and architecture "ambiguate" and demand more than one valid interpretation. Over and over he stresses *the artist's instinct to join contrary principles in one union*. . . . Steinberg comments that "reconciling contrariety pervades the design," that "coincident opposites abound in the picture," that "Leonardo elaborates to *bring opposites into states of union*." . . . [Steinberg] speaks of "a billeting of incompatible presences . . . *under one roof*," of a symmetry of cancellations," and a "concord of contradictions . . . the principle of reciprocal counterchange," . . . "the physique of contrary principles."[28]

As it stands, the multiplist can agree with Steinberg as to the multiple interpretability of the painting. But the multiplist would require that the painting be treated as a single work answering to multiple interpretations—each interpretation counted separately on account of their mutual incongruence. Maxwell affirms that we should understand it as a case of a single work answering to a *single* hyphenated admissible interpretation, where we should take the Betrayal and Eucharist interpretations as one. Steinberg's strategy of "absorption under one roof" does give credence to Maxwell's reading. The result is that incongruence is allowed *within* a given interpretation.

In contrast, Podro's account more persuasively suggests that we should count the two interpretations as two and he invites us to switch between them. Maxwell is mistaken to think that Podro's reconciliationist intervention results in aggregating interpretations. He is mistaken to think that a singularist condition results. Maxwell says, given Podro's intervention:

> The true meaning of the *Last Supper,* in short, is bound up, not just with the existence of two, equally valid, different interpretations (betrayal and Eucharist), but with the way in which these two readings interact with one another, or are related to each other, in the form of the picture. The correct . . . interpretation will incorporate all the meanings.[29]

Contrary to Maxwell's aim, Podro is not advancing a single comprehensive ("under one roof") interpretation but a strategy for interaction between interpretations. Podro recommends that the Betrayal and the Eucharist interpretations should interact and relate to one another, presumably in Gestalt-switch fashion. He invites us to move alternatively between incongruent interpretations. His is no new, single, over-arching interpretation, but an invitation to switch back and forth between different interpretations. Interaction is not conjunction. So understood, a multiplist condition remains in which incongruence obtains between interpretations instead of within a single hyphenated interpretation. For Podro, no aggregation of interpretations would have been installed.

But in order to satisfy his general (perpetual) singularism, Maxwell would need to affirm that for *any* would-be incongruent interpretations, they should be aggregated. His strategy commits him to the improbable claim that in no cases is there incongruence *between* interpretations. All incongruence must be internal within a single overarching interpretation.

11. Meta-Singularism and Meta-Multiplism

The idea of an overarching interpretation gives rise to questions concerning second-order or "meta" consideration. At a meta level, a meta-singularist will say that singularism itself is *singularly true.* And at a meta level the meta-multiplist will say that multiplism is reasonable or true—depending on whether the very theses of singularism and multiplism themselves are taken by the multiplist to be among those that answer to more than one interpretation. But a meta-multiplist cannot allow singularism, since the second is cast in a universal form. Accordingly, the distinction between singularism and multiplism is "level-relative." We could generate meta levels indefinitely.

In face of such open-endedness, we might be tempted to stop the generation of levels by holding that, in the end, when all meta levels are exhausted, one interpretation trumps the others. We may call someone who asserts singularism at this final, God's eye level, a "super-singularist." Correspondingly, we may call one who asserts multiplism at this final God's eye level a "super-multiplist."

The idea of a God's eye point of view does not entail super-singularism. For perhaps God is multiplist with respect to God's multiplism. A super-multiplist could hold that from God's eye point of view, multiplism rules. Accordingly, a super-multiplist would see the super-singularist as having overshot the interpretive demands of God. As regards interpretive demands, God might be more liberal than the singularist imagines. God may have left the matter quite open. In short, no reason exists that God must be singularist.

Regardless, I suggest that *the positing of a super level* or *super frame* is ad hoc and arbitrary. I find no reason to assume that the generation of levels must stop, there being no finality about it. We are *always already* situated in ongoing practices in which meta-levels are routinely relativized as object-level subjects with respect to more abstracted meta-levels. Accordingly, instead of stipulating an ad hoc final level, we should pursue the distinction between singularism and multiplism at levels that accord with our interests and purposes as we encounter them.

Both singularism and multiplism deploy the concept of *ideal admissibility*. The notion of ideal admissibility might (misleadingly) be thought to presuppose the idea of an *end of inquiry*. Yet we should understand the idea of an end of inquiry in pragmatic terms wherein informed practitioners may agree that all pertinent considerations are available to make a suitably informed determination of whether a given object of interpretation answers to one or more than one interpretation. We should understand pertinent ideals as limiting concepts, within provisional, unfolding, and changing interpretive conditions.

Two

SINGULARISM, MULTIPLISM, AND THEIR DIFFERENCES

1. The Incompatibility of Singularist and Multiplist Conditions

Consider the following two statements: (1) For any object of interpretation only one single ideally admissible interpretation exists (singularist thesis); and (2) For some objects of interpretation, more than one interpretation is ideally admissible (multiplist thesis). I assert that these statements are mutually contradictory. More pointedly, I assert that *any given object of interpretation cannot simultaneously answer to a singularist and a multiplist condition.* This appears straightforward enough.

Yet, Bernard Harrison and Patricia Hanna hold that one and the same object of interpretation can simultaneously answer to both a singularist and a multiplist condition. How would this be possible? They argue their case in relation to the example of the practice of measurement:

> There can be no such thing as the real length of anything, because there can be no such thing as length determined without reference to some modulus or other. We cannot speak, because it makes no sense, of length tout court, but only of length-in-inches, or in-microns.[1]

On their account, length exists only in some modulus or reference frames, such as in inches or in microns. Where more than one reference frame exists, more than one result is admissible. In that case, apparently, a multiplist condition obtains. At the same time, for a given reference frame, the length of a physical object can answer to only one admissible interpretation. For example, this table is *n* inches long, and not another number. In this case, a singularist condition obtains. Given these premises, both a multiplist and singularist condition appears to obtain.

Yet, we must ask whether a plurality of reference frames does entail a multiplist condition. If pertinent reference frames were inter-translatable without residue, they would appear to be congruent. So they would not count as two reference frames, but as one. Inches and microns are mutually translatable without residue. A formula exists that translates between inches and microns without residue. An inch is defined as 2.54 centimeters exactly, and a micron is 1/10,000th of a centimeter exactly. An inch is 25,400 microns exactly. No irrational numbers are involved. No residues result. So, it appears, Harrison and Hanna's example of a multiplist condition amounts to a singularist and not a multiplist case. At first it appears to fail to exemplify the multiplist side of their joint singularist-multiplist assertion.

In response to this argument, Hanna effectively replies that because an inch is translatable into microns is irrelevant to the issue of incongruence, and so irrelevant to the question of their numerical identity.[2] She argues that the propriety of invoking one or another reference frame on different occasions is the relevant element. To invoke inches is appropriate on some occasions and inappropriate on others. Measuring a picture frame, for example, in inches is appropriate, while doing so in microns is inappropriate—even if inches are fully translatable into microns. Measuring sub-atomic particles in inches is inappropriate, even if inches are fully translatable into microns. In short, incongruence of these reference frames obtains at the level of the *propriety of use*. When such incongruence obtains, a multiplist condition obtains. Note that the propriety of use of one reference frame or another reflects interests and purposes that motivate the choice of some sort of project. The interest in having a painting hung well on a wall, for example, motivates the project of hanging it appropriately. Hanging the picture suggests the propriety of measuring the painting and the wall in inches as opposed to microns.

Hanna's reply to my "translatability" argument is a welcome contribution. It unseats my initial thought that intertranslatability guarantees congruence of use and that where translatability obtains, no plurality of reference frames obtains. It undercuts my initial claim that translatability disallows counting otherwise two reference frames as one.

But we must ask whether she holds fixed the same object of interpretation in each case when she moves between inches and microns. I will return to this question presently.

2. Precision and Accuracy: A Misleading Turn

First, though, consider a byway that Hanna pursues. To buttress her counterargument against my translatability argument, she claims that inches and microns are not intertranslatable. She suggests that we should not count them as one reference frame, because measuring in inches and microns reflects different *standards of precision*. This precision argument is distinct from the propriety in use argument. But the precision argument fails. Hanna argues as follows:

> Imagine that I have a scale model of the Moon, complete with all its craters. I have no present use for it and want to store it in my attic; to this end, I want to see if it will actually fit in the available space. I ask my husband, Dudley, to measure the circumference, handing him a measuring tape from my sewing kit. He does so and tells me that it's 9 feet around. In the meantime, I've received a call asking me to make an impression of the "equator" of my model; something out of latex approxi-

mately 2 inches wide. But, the caller warns me, "I'm on a limited budget, so could you please give me a very precise indication of just how much latex this will take? " At this point, Dudley suggests that we need a measurement that will give us greater precision than we can achieve with the measuring tape. He suggests that we use microns. The result of this, second, measurement is that the circumference is 3,048,000 microns. Using the formula "1 inch = 25,400 microns," this converts to 10 feet.[3]

Hanna's example does not show that a difference in precision between inches and microns exists. The difference in the results of measuring arises from an equivocation on what the circumference measurement is. The results differ because what is measured is different. The respective results can be equally precise. In the first case, the circumference does not include details of the craters. In the second case, the circumference includes details of the craters. The requests in both these cases are requests for different things.

More generally, Hanna seeks to distinguish precision from accuracy. To do so, she contrasts the inches marked on her measuring tape with microns, presuming that microns are more precise than inches. But the contrast is not shown by her example. The pertinent contrast is between inches and microns (which are intertranslatable), not between marks on a sewing kit tape and microns. *Applications* of reference frames may be more or less accurate, without altering the fact that inches and microns are equally precise. She confuses a degree of precision between inches and microns with a degree of precision in an application procedure. We must not confuse an inaccurate measuring tape which may be "good enough" for sewing and other purposes with a putative imprecision of inches. Inches are every bit as precise as microns. Microns and inches are precisely inter-translatable.

To be sure, it may be *accurate* to say that the doorway through which the model is to pass is, say, four foot-lengths long (Hanna's example), or four times the lengths of the measuring agent's foot. But since a foot-length is not constant—the length of the agent's foot might change in hot weather, for example, and the length varies according to the particular agent doing the measuring—the notion of four foot-lengths is not precise. In contrast, the reference frames of inches and microns remain precise. Techniques of measurement are not, after all, what has been identified as the reference frame. Inches and microns are. Again, these are equally precise, even if—to suit different purposes—the techniques of measurement are sometimes more rigorously applied than others. So different interests and purposes may motivate different techniques of measurement. The reference frames do not become imprecise. Length is always expressed in a reference frame and interests and purposes—along with the technique of measurement appropriate to those interests and purposes—suggest what degree of accuracy is appropriate. But, it does not follow that the reference frames—inches and microns—vary in their precision.

3. Back from the Turn

I turn now to points of substantial agreement. With Harrison and Hanna, I agree that:

> Absent a modulus in terms of which O is to be measured, the question [whether it answers to a singularist or multiplist condition] cannot be answered. . . . Once we are provided with a modulus, we see that the original question [of the range of ideally admissible interpretations] does not, indeed cannot, require a unique answer. . . . The only obvious reply available is that there must be a final, unique truth about every property of anything that can be regarded as an existing constituent of reality, a final truth about the dimensional properties of things. The intelligibility of this claim is precisely what is at issue. . . . [no] final, unique truth about every property of anything that can be regarded as an existing constituent of reality, a final truth about the dimensional properties of things . . . whether a given object of interpretation answers to multiplism, or to singularism, or to both, may be a function not of its nature, but of that of the practice through which we interrogate it. . . .[4]

I further agree that:

> In the case of a "cultural" object, that object may answer equally to singularism or to multiplism, depending on the nature, not of the object, but of that of the questions we put to it and of the practices that give point to those questions by supplying us with the means of resolving them.[5]

In light of these agreements, let us return to our initial question whether a given object of interpretation may simultaneously answer to a singularist and a multiplist condition. If an object of interpretation answers to a singularist condition, can it be the same as that which answers to a multiplist condition? We might be tempted to reply (although Harrison and Hanna do not) that the pre-praxial worldly "stuff" of an object of interpretation might satisfy a multiplist condition. Yet even if we could have access to this further stuff, we would have no reason to believe it to be determinately countable or countable as *one*.

Interpretations might be thought indirectly to address themselves to an undifferentiated uncountable world. But the undifferentiated world is not the same as its differentiated objects. A singularist condition may obtain with respect to objects as differentiated by pertinent reference frames. We would be mistaken, though, to think that a multiplist condition could obtain with respect to the undifferentiated world. Not only is such a world uncountable, but it could not qualify as the common thing that is supposed to answer to a singularist and a multiplist condition. We cannot assume that the undifferentiated uncountable world can satisfy the multiplist side of Harrison and

Hanna's dual claim. For, being uncountable, it does not satisfy the multiplist's requirement that a *single* object of interpretation answers to more than one admissible interpretation. To satisfy the multiplist side of their dual claim, Harrison and Hanna would need to hold that it does. They would also need to say that it—singularly *it*—can answer to more than one admissible interpretation. But no uncountable world can count as a single object of interpretation. The condition of commonality of objects of interpretation addressed by otherwise contesting interpretations would, at that level, fail. So, with that failure, the interpretive ideals of singularism and multiplism could not—at the same level—simultaneously apply. I have mentioned this possible argument from pre-praxial stuff to set it aside. Harrison and Hanna do not advance this argument.

We may ask whether that which is described in inches can be the same thing as that described in microns. I suggest that we cannot answer the question of sameness of objects of interpretation by an inspection of some presumed object independent of practices. Harrison and Hanna are right to hold that "the choice [whether a singularist or multiplist condition obtains] depends not on the type of object whose nature we are concerned to interpret, but on the structure of the linguistic practice through which our interrogation of the object under interpretation is conducted."[6] I agree further that:

> A literary, or religious, or aesthetic tradition develops by reinterpretation, and as reinterpretations multiply and cohere into new structures of response or belief, so the entities that populate the discourses of culture change their nature or divide amoebically into daughter-entities.[7]

Significantly, Harrison and Hanna endorse the thought that objects of interpretation may change their identities—"amoebically," as they say, as between reference frames. But if they may do so, is it the same object of interpretation that persists as between reference frames? If "daughter-entities" are not their "mother-entities," however closely related, how can they be the same objects of interpretation?

In keeping with Harrison and Hanna's praxial view, I hold that the identity of an object of interpretation is made determinate or are stabilized by the terms of a pertinent reference frame. Yet once a pertinent reference frame has fixed its object's identity conditions, that object cannot answer to both a singularist and a multiplist condition.

The table as a table is a middle-sized object. We can say the table is hard. Yet, understood in terms of microstructures, a shift in reference frames occurs such that the newly instantiated object no longer answers to such predicates as hardness. Strictly speaking, the object is no longer a table. In this way, changes of reference frames result in changes in the identity of objects of interpretation.

No determinate pre-praxial fact of the matter exists about the identity of what would become of the product of practices. For example, no determinate fact of the matter as to how large a room is independent of an inquirer's interests and purposes exists. Is the length of the room that which is indicated by its blueprints? Is it the room bounded by its walls? Which walls, the interior or exterior walls? Does it include living space, excluding or including the trim around the windows and doors? Does it include or exclude the carpeting? Does it include the walls with or without one or several coats of paint or no coats of paint? Do we require that the room be measured at some designated temperature? Without answers to these sorts of questions we have no determinate answer to the question of the length of the room.

Which questions we ask is a matter of interests and purposes. But, if we grant that no interest-independent answer to the question of the length of the room exists, are we not still speaking of the same room? Well, that depends (as in the case of the table) upon our interests and purposes. But once we agree that we are talking about the same thing, it cannot answer to both a singularist and multiplist condition. The plurality of answers to the question of the length of the room amounts to a multiplist condition with respect a single room, a single object of interpretation. Yet if we identify the object of interpretation, say in terms of microstructures, and shift its identity, we may have an object of interpretation that answers to a singularist condition. It remains that a shift of object of interpretation does not mandate that for a given object of interpretation (before and after the shift), we are addressing the same thing that simultaneously answers to a singularist and multiplist condition. Put otherwise, a given object of interpretation cannot simultaneously answer to a singularist and a multiplist condition. When it appears that it does, we should search for differences in interpretive projects and reference frames. Differences in such projects and reference frames mandate differences in objects of interpretation. When I say that the table is sixty inches long and that a cluster of micro structures is 1,525,000 microns long (60 x 25,400), I signal that we are measuring different sorts of things. No determinate sort of thing is *there*, independent of reference frames, which would serve different interpretive projects.

Consider yet another example. "This is a book," is no pre-praxial fact of the matter. Not only is the singularity of the book post-praxial, but that the object is a *book*, is post-praxial. The designation of "book" carries with it the usually unacknowledged understanding that it is a middle-sized object and not a microstructure. Yet we could see it otherwise, depending upon our interests and purposes. No fact of the matter about what we are pointing to exists. The identity of objects of interpretation is a product of practices. No fact of the matter about pre-praxial identity exists. That over which interpretations might compete is, itself, an interpretive achievement.

More generally, the world awaits individuation or objectification within pertinent practices. After such individuation or objectification, its objects are not the same as the world—not because we cannot have access to the world, but because it makes no sense to ask of a pre-praxial world if *it* is the same as its individuated iterations. For the question of sameness can arise only after praxial individuation has been instituted.

So understood, no general criterion for the identity of objects of interpretation exists *there* to be had before the appropriate application of reference frames.[8] The question of sameness of objects of interpretation is not a matter of their being pliable, flexible, elastic, malleable, or the like. Whether one or two Chinas or one or two Koreas actually exist is not a matter of China's or Korea's being *pliable* or the like. Whether my self is one or more is not a matter of its being pliable, but a matter of pertinent reference frames in which my self is nested.

Arguments often arise about which reference frame we should invoke. But the lines of those arguments are different from those whose interlocutors think they are talking about a fact of the matter independent of reference frames that set identity conditions.

Once we have fixed the terms of identity by one or another reference frame, it remains that its objects of interpretation cannot simultaneously answer to only one and more than one admissible interpretation. When even it appears so (contra Harrison and Hanna), we should take such appearance as an occasion to look for an equivocation in or between the operative reference frames.

These are my misgivings about Harrison and Hanna's claim that a singularist and a multiplist condition may simultaneously obtain with respect to a common object of interpretation. Even so, such misgivings do not diminish my agreement with their constructive realism (or their relative realism, as they call it) which I will discuss in chapter seven.

4. Practical Differences between Singularism and Multiplism

We might ask what practical difference it makes to embrace either singularism or multiplism. The multiplist who says, "I choose this interpretation over others and I have good reasons for doing so, but I allow that certain others are also admissible," displays a conduct of inquiry quite different from that of the singularist who says, " I choose this interpretation over others and I have good reasons for doing so, but I disallow that others are also admissible."

Consider the case of a singularist mediator in a dispute such as that between Israelis and Palestinians, or between Irish Protestants and Catholics, or between Indian Hindus and Moslems. Or, consider the case of a singularist counselor who seeks to help reconcile two estranged partners. Presumably, a singularist mediator or therapist would guide discussions toward eliciting pertinent facts with the aim of arriving at the single right interpretation and to chart a course of dialogue or action in accord with it.

In contrast, presumably, a multiplist would seek to reveal the reasonableness, appropriateness, or aptness of each party's story, and to suggest to each party that they consider the reasonableness of the other's story, without assuming that there must be one and only one admissible story. The singularist and multiplist exhibit distinct conducts of inquiry as they treat such cases.

But we might urge that these are not cases of trying to "get the story right." Instead, these might be cases of trying to put that question aside—to "dispose" of it, as Nancy Weston would say, to achieve another aim, namely to foster peace or to heal. The political, religious, or domestic mediator-counselor might be less interested in settling upon which interpretations of the respective situations are admissible, or whether the range of admissible interpretations is singularist or multiplist. They might be more interested in getting on with living together in peace. That might mean exiting from the discussion of admissible interpretations altogether. It might involve the pursuit of aims other than or beyond elucidation.

The mediator may embrace reconciliation or healing as a long-term aim. Yet insofar as such reconciliation or healing depends upon satisfactory elucidatory inquiries into the admissibility of interpretations of pertinent situations, the conducts of inquiry associated with singularist and multiplist ideals would be operative. (See chapter ten.)

Further, when considering these sorts of cases, a plurality of interpretations is up for consideration. That plurality is taken by the singularist mediator as an *interim condition*, interim in the sense that "at the end of inquiry" one admissible interpretation will remain. To that end, the singularist understands the inquiry to proceed. Yet the multiplist mediator takes that plurality as an *ineliminable condition*. The singularist's and the multiplist's conducts of inquiry are affected by their respective understanding about the nature of the inquiry in which they are engaged.

5. Overshooting

Singularists and multiplists will have different attitudes toward institutions which demand singularist verdicts. Practical or political demands may force us to "overshoot" inconclusive grounds. Some legal institutions, for example, require a singularist verdict in the face of characteristically multiplist conditions. Legal institutions characteristically mandate singularist verdicts even when available evidence is inconclusive. While the short-term inconclusivity of evidence in the face of mandated singularist verdicts is compatible with either singularism or multiplism, singularist and multiplist attitudes about this fact differ. A singularist will regard those institutional mandates to be appropriate but precipitous with respect to warranting evidence. On the other hand, a multiplist will regard such institutional mandates not so much as precipitous, as inappropriate, with respect to warranting evidence—even if practical demands require closure. For example, Nancy Weston remarks:

In a standard court case, only one judgment, endorsing one interpretation of the events at issue, is possible: a criminal defendant is either found guilty or is acquitted; a civil suit is decided either for the plaintiff or for the civil defendant. . . . [T]his state of affairs appears to constitute an institutional constraint that mandates singularism. The trial court issues its singular judgment despite encountering a lack of conclusiveness in the reasons offered to support the interpretation of the case given by one side or the other of the dispute. This lack of conclusiveness, such as follows from ambiguities and incompleteness in the process of proof, may be understood as contingent and regrettable, if chronic, compatibly with singularism; or as intrinsic and appropriate, compatibly with multiplism, although it will then appear incongruous and *insupportable that multiplism is abandoned for singularism in the court's final judgment.*[9]

Both singularists and multiplists agree that verdicts need to be pronounced. Singularists find it regrettable that a singularist verdict is chronically demanded prematurely. In contrast, multiplists find it regrettable (if necessary) that some institutions mandate a singularist verdict. The demands made by such institutions falsify the realities of the evidential situation. This difference translates into normative stances toward institutional demands. The multiplist attitude tends to be more skeptical of institutional (singularist) demands.

Weston does observe that the law is compliant. In some sorts of cases, the law allows for degrees of accountability in accord with degrees of inconclusivity. Yet even here, accountability is assigned in accord with parceled or split charges, each again answered by a singularist verdict. Weston says:

In splitting its verdict, the jury may be understood to decline its singularist mandate; yet the means by which it may do so directly—as by confessing itself to be unable to reach a decision (a "hung" jury"), or by determining different counts, charges, or claims for different parties . . . (perhaps an instance of singularist pluralism)—are perfectly acceptable. . . .[10]

For the sake of closure, a "leap" or an overshooting results from inconclusive grounds to actions. That leap is demanded—perhaps for reasons of "disposition," as Weston puts it—by virtue of power bestowed upon the judge or jury:

[Given] multiple "right answers," the court's pronouncement of a singular answer comes to appear illegitimate, an insupportably excessive status bestowed willfully upon one resolution selected by the court from among the class of equally admissible and inconclusive alternatives. . . . The determination of law by the court and the resolution of a case on its basis thus come to be understood as merely an exercise of power instead of as the discernment and pronouncement of right.[11]

As Weston suggests, desire or need to close the matter, to *dispose* of the question characteristically motivates such overshooting:

> When we demand such . . . [an] authority as a "single overarching standard that will adjudicate between claims to rightness," what we crave and require is, above all, disposition: We wish, not merely for an answer to the question of rightness . . . but instead for an answer of a quite particular sort, namely one that will *dispose* of the question, answering it conclusively so that we may be done with it and with any duty to attend to it further. We want relief from the question, and from the responsibility for determining right; . . . we can make that claim only because our demand for authoritative determinability and disposition presumes rightness to be extraneous to the matter itself. There thus arises an apparent vacuum of rightness, into which we step as its creators.[12]

At this juncture we might think that the authority for disposition to bring or "force" the matter to a close must be arbitrary and a matter of sheer exercise of power. Yet we have no reason to assume it must be arbitrarily or without warrant. Again, Weston observes:

> The judicial decision, like the litigants' actions and the lawyers' arguments, is now understood to have the character of a choice among preferences, to be determined by the consultation and comparison of advantages yielded by different resolutions for the satisfaction of desire. That such desire may be altruistic, as with public interest advocacy, or responsive to collective or social preference instead of to the judge's personal preference, does not alter this preferential character or diminish its pervasiveness, for even the selection of such a ground as determinative of one's actions is itself understood to be a matter of preference.[13]

Even the exercise of preference being pervasive neither means that choices between inconclusive interpretations (and their subsequent consequences) are arbitrary or whimsical, nor puts the range of admissible interpretations on a preferential par.

The legal case also exemplifies different attitudes about decisiveness. A multiplist might decisively champion a given interpretation over other competitors while conceding that they are multiply admissible. Decisiveness and indecisiveness are attitudes with which persons embrace an interpretation. They concern degrees of resolve. We might think that the degree of resolve to champion a given interpretation should always accord with the degree of its conclusiveness, that one should not overshoot warranting grounds. But, as in the legal case, we may allow decisiveness without conclusiveness. Andreea Deciu Ritivoi, for example, observes:

Granted, in multiplist cases such reasons should not be so strong as to unseat all alternatives as inadmissible, but that does not mean that multiplism is some-how [sic] ethically indecisive or argumentatively feeble. When situations demand it, multiplism can express a rigorous ethical and argumentative stance.[14]

Correspondingly—in cases of weakness of will or indecision, for example—we may allow indecisiveness with conclusiveness. More generally, we may allow indecisiveness to go with conclusiveness. The degree of decisiveness often overshoots the degree of conclusiveness—sometimes for practical or political reasons—as for example, when circumstances mandate action before anything like a complete inventory of appropriate warranting grounds could have been considered. Degree of warrant need not accord with strength of resolve.

Within a given contest conclusive grounds might exist to unseat all but one admissible interpretation. But no "super" or "imperial" contest that would adjudicate or hierarchize between all contests can exist. A "super-singularist" may postulate an imperial standard under which all interests and purposes, projects, interpretations, and their objects of interpretation may be ranked, as in a totalized scheme of valuation. But such a postulation can be nothing more than a dream, for the multiplicity of such interests, purposes, and the rest is irreducible and ineliminable. As Weston says:

> There is . . . no suprahistorical position to which we might retreat for authoritative or final determination of these matters, as theory envisions, and no ready comparison as with other times and cultures . . . from which we might extract a theoretical diagnosis.[15]

In this chapter I rehearsed the distinction between singularism and multiplism. I have argued that these interpretive ideals are logically incompatible, and that a given object of interpretation—once appropriately identified within a reference frame—cannot simultaneously answer to a singularist and a multiplist condition. While I found Harrison and Hanna's arguments against the exclusivity of singularism and multiplism wanting, I found their deployment of the idea of a modulus—which I have generalized as a reference frame—to be fruitful. I indicated the practical differences between singularism and multiplism as regards the conducts of inquiry suggested by each, including their applications in the case of the law. Finally, I rejected the super-singularist's dream of imperial grounds for the conclusive adjudication between all interpretations.

Three

ON THE IDEA OF MULTIPLISM

1. Singularism vs. Multiplism:
A Putative Collapse of the Distinction

David Crocker seeks to unseat the distinction between singularism and multiplism by focusing on that provision of multiplism, which asserts that, of admissible interpretations, we may have reasons for embracing a preferred interpretation without lapsing into a singularist condition. He argues that reasons for preferred admissible interpretations amount to grounds for ranking to a limit of one. He concludes that the distinction between singularism and multiplism collapses. If reasons can disqualify competing interpretations as inadmissible, no difference in kind would exist between multiplism and singularism. He says, "Perhaps the singularist's one admissible interpretation comes to no more than the multiplist's most preferable interpretation."[1] More fully, he says:

> [Michael] Krausz insists that operating under the multiplist ideal is compatible with "countenancing one interpretation as preferable (for good reasons) over other admissible interpretations." We might ask whether this multiplist accommodation to singularism does not go too far, since it appears to accept one and only one interpretation as preferable and that there need exist any theoretical or practical differences between multiplist preferability among admissible alternatives and singularist exclusive admissibility is not evident. Perhaps the singularist's one admissible interpretation comes to no more than the multiplist's most preferable interpretation. In short, Krausz's sharp distinction might collapse into two points on a continuum (determined by degree of preferability supplied by reasons).[2]

Yet I suggest that a person can prefer one of several admissible interpretations, supported by justifying reasons without resulting in a singularist condition. Vibha Chaturvedi illustrates this point when she asks:

> Can we say that good reasons exist for preferring one interpretation to others as implied by multiplism? Let me take the case of different interpretations of the same sacred text. You might say that if an interpretation can competently explain or account for the whole text or most of the text, that interpretation is preferable to others that fail to do so. But to

expect that the preferred interpretation must account *for the essential or more significant parts* of the text is reasonable, even if it fails to do so with respect to large sections of the not so essential parts. *There can be difference of opinion about what constitutes essential or most crucial parts.* So long as the differing interpretations are outcomes of the same interpretive apparatus, we can give reasons for favoring one over others.[3]

In short, an interpretation may be justified with reasons as more preferable over another because it accounts for "the essential or more significant parts" of the text. But what is salient, "essential," or "more significant" is characteristically contestable.

One reason for assigning salience to some features of a work is that doing so helps illuminate a story about the identified properties holistically presented. Yet different people with different interests and purposes (deploying different apparatuses, as Chaturvedi says) may identify different properties as salient, prompting not just another story but another story about a different set of properties configured in different holistic patterns of significance. Strictly speaking, such disagreement about salience or significance would result not in competition between two stories about a fully common object of interpretation. Instead, the disagreement might involve a difference as to what we *should* assume to be the object of interpretation.

2. Ampliative and Determinative Reasons

In response to Crocker, I introduce a distinction between *ampliative* and *determinative* reasons. Accordingly, we may have ampliative reasons for preferring one admissible interpretation over another without such reasons being so strong as to disallow other admissible interpretations. An *ampliative* reason does not seek to persuade, but to amplify, fill in, explicate, or provide the rationale why someone holds the view that he or she does. It provides understanding for why someone embraces the view she does. Ampliative reasons enlarge upon, ramify, or demonstrate a narrative coherence of a view on offer. They seek not to persuade an interlocutor over to one's side. Such reasons are more conversational than argumentative. In contrast, a *determinative* reason seeks to determine the outcome of a contest between contending views. Persons invoke determinative reasons to persuade their interlocutors of the superiority of their view over others. Determinative reasons are meant to persuade the interlocutor of the rightness of the view on offer.

We more usually think of reasons in the determinative sense. But we have no reason to disallow perhaps more prevalent ampliative reasons. Both sorts of reasons may operate at the same time. A determinative reason may be offered in addition to an ampliative reason, which may amount to saying that a position once understood—via ampliative reasons—may be trumped in a discussion about whether we *should* embrace or adopt the amplified position. Yet sometimes to engage in a determinative discussion at all is inappropriate.

For example, we may ask why someone embraces a Vedantic view of self-realization. The account offered in reply may articulate the Vedantic rationale; it may show how we`might see the point of doing so without attempting to convince someone else to adopt that view. Or, we may ask someone why he or she keeps kosher. The account offered in reply may articulate a rationale for doing so without attempting to convince someone else to adopt that practice. Such reasons are ampliative. When, though, such an activity is further joined by reasons why someone *should* adopt that practice, to convince someone that doing so is better than not doing so, then the reasons thereby invoked are determinative.

The distinction between ampliative and determinative reasons allows us to see the difference between multiplism and "critical pluralism." Critical pluralism holds that all preference between admissible interpretations is a matter of unreasoned whimsy. In contrast, multiplism holds that preference between admissible interpretations may be a matter of ampliative reasons.

Further, where ampliative, not determinative reasons apply, thinking that all multiplist conditions collapse into singularist conditions is a mistake. On Crocker's account, reasons that justify preferences amongst admissible interpretations hierarchize them. This may be so of determinative reasons, but not of ampliative reasons. Ampliative reasons do not, in themselves, hierarchize. At the same time, they provide a minimal rationality which goes beyond the mere whimsical expression of preferences.

Crocker is wrong to suggest that if multiplism allows for preferences with good reasons, the distinction between singularism and multiplism collapses. On his account, all reason-giving amounts to hierarchizing candidate interpretations. Yet ampliative reasons do not do so. At the same time, they provide a rationality which goes beyond the mere whimsical expression of preferences. Since ampliative reasons may foreclose whimsical preference between admissible interpretations but still not unseat alternative interpretations, the distinction between multiplism and critical pluralism is sustained. Ampliative reasons are strong enough and weak enough to sustain the distinction between singularism and multiplism. Harrison and Hanna rightly say:

> good grounds may exist in a particular case for preferring a measurement in inches over one in microns; but in no such case will such grounds be conclusive, identifying one or the other as the only correct one.[4]

Further, good grounds may exist for preferring one reference frame over another, without such grounds being conclusive. No hierarchical ranking of one reference frame over another one exists. Yet, within a given reference frame, a single admissible interpretation may or may not exist. The choice between reference frames may be justified by pertinent interests and purposes.

As Nelson Goodman's example will show (see chapter five), for different interests and purposes (issuing in different projects), we may hold the sun as fixed or the earth as fixed. But once we hold the earth as fixed, we may say a driver is speeding over the speed limit. Yet before invoking a reference frame, a driver is neither speeding nor not speeding. While we may choose to hold the earth as fixed or as unfixed—depending on our interests and purposes—it does not follow that the driver is both speeding and not speeding simultaneously.

Notice that multiplism—understood as a generally defined ideal—is satisfied if, in a single reference frame, more than one interpretation is admissible. Multipism is also satisfied if only one interpretation within each reference frame is admissible but more than one reference frames is admissible. These conditions hold only if pertinent interpretations address the same thing.

3. Dialogical Space

Our stating ampliative reasons to others does assume that our interlocutor shares with us a dialogical space. It assumes that others can understand us and that shared understanding in both directions is possible. Under some circumstances, on the other hand, understanding may legitimately be one way. Or, sometimes, as a tactical matter, a person may feign non-understanding. Alternatively, a person may refuse to extend dialogical imagination as a matter of power politics and refuse to take the other's view seriously. Yet by allowing a dialogical space between us, we need not assume that we construe the dialogical space per se in a singularist or multiplist manner.

For us to share and mutually grasp ampliative reasons with one another, no full incommensurability between interlocutors can exist. When hearing ampliative reasons of another person, we are not merely hearing acoustical sounds or looking at mere inscriptions on a page. We grasp what they are uttering by virtue of our ability to imagine ourselves in their place. Yet, ineliminably, we do so from our place in our own reference frame. That means neither that we make the other's reference frame our own, nor that we abandon our own.

Further, a reference frame is characteristically *adumbrant*. While determining what is "in" and what is "out" of a given reference frame is not a simple matter (there may be no clean cuts between them), we may differentiate them. For example, while no clean line separates "Russian" from "Ukrainian" cultures, they most assuredly are differentiable.

I have suggested that the possibility of disagreement presupposes that contestants agree that they are talking about the same thing. If contestants disagree about whether they are talking about the same thing, they must disagree about whether they disagree. Within a given tradition, a difference of opinion may exist as to whether contestants are talking about the same thing. In her treatment of the Hindu case, Chaturvedi notes:

Here the object of interpretation is under dispute. But wherever the object is the same we are confronted with real multiplism. Within the Hindu tradition an example of diversity of interpretations of the same object can be seen with regard to different viewpoints of *Vedanta*. The term "Vedanta" means "the final portions of the *Vedas,*" namely the *Upanisads.* It has come to signify "the settled conclusions of the *Vedas* taken as a whole." As far as the *Purva-Mimamsa* school is concerned, it can be said that it addresses a different object, namely a different part of the *Veda.* But the different schools of Vedanta refer to the same *sruti.*[5]

According to Chaturvedi, within the Hindu tradition (broadly understood), disagreement exists about what is being addressed as the object of interpretation—the Vedas as a whole or parts of the Veda. While the viewpoints are aimed toward a similar general text, they focus their attention on different objects of interpretation.

Interpreters of a common tradition may start by agreeing with each other that they are addressing the same thing. But upon analysis, they may find that they are not. They may come to "pluralize" their object of interpretation. This does not preclude the possibility that an interpreter of one tradition may discover that an interpreter of another tradition is addressing the same thing as he or she is. This second possibility would involve overcoming the idiosyncrasies of each tradition that under other circumstances represent a barrier in translation between the traditions.

Complex relationships obtain within and across traditions. Some interpreters within a given tradition may agree that they are talking about the same thing while others in the same tradition may disagree. Some interpreters of different traditions may agree that they are talking about the same thing, while others (again of different traditions) may disagree. Still others, of either of these traditions, may observe that the grounds for either agreement or disagreement in the above cases do not obtain. The agreement or disagreement about whether interpreters are talking about the same thing cannot serve as a criterion for the sameness or difference of traditions.

Four

INTENTIONALITY AND ITS OBJECTS

The phrase, "objects of interpretation," can misleadingly suggest a discourse of material substance. We should resist such a reading. An object of interpretation is an intentional object endowed with meaning within pertinent reference frames or practices. Accordingly, the phrase object of interpretation designates no object in a substantive or material sense. Objects of interpretation are already represented, which is to say that we understand them in terms of some reference frame. No objects of interpretation that are not already represented in some way exist. No uninterpreted objects of interpretation exist. An object of *interpretation* is already seen *as* something or other. As Paul Thom says, "for an act of interpretation to occur, there must be an intentional object but there may or may not be an external object."[1]

A reference frame endows meaning or significance to an intentional object. The frame provides pertinent interpretive norms. For example, in soccer the difference between kicking a ball into a net and scoring a point is a difference in reference frame. The game of soccer provides rules for appropriate behavior. The difference between a piece of paper and a dollar bill is that the dollar bill has been bestowed meaning or value by virtue of an assumed reference frame of a monetary system. In this way, the identity of an intentional object implicates a reference frame in which it is nested. We might worry that frame-relativity makes the "assignment" of identity by frames to be subjective. The worry is needless, for frame-relativity is no more subjective than scoring a point in a game of soccer or the assignment of the value to a dollar bill.

We cannot make sense of intentional phenomena independent of the historically constituted practices in which they are found and fostered. The meanings of objects of interpretation are constituted by their relations to pertinent norms. Within such a field, we assign salience to some features of intentional phenomena. In this way, we may see a figure *as* a face or *as* a vase. Or, we may see a painting *as* representational or *as* abstract. When we see the figure or the painting *as* an *a* or *as* a *b*, we do so as a product of an intentional act. Ronald Moore puts the point this way:

> Practices . . . provide the aims and orientations of their ingredient programs; they set the range of admissible solutions to the problem-situations they engage and orient practitioners to those features of a given domain of inquiry that are significant and salient. . . . These socially rooted interactions provide the appropriate *contextual matrix* for the stories we tell about our selves and others; and through them the issue of "which stories will do" gets resolved. The admissibility of possi-

bilities is a function of human practices. Our stories are tied to our projects, and these projects are developed within, and make sense in, communicative social settings. Just as there can be no private language, there can be no intelligible private stories, and no private art.[2]

The acts of seeing *as* are what (according to Moore) Virgil Aldrich calls "acts of aspection" according to which we see a thing:

> first as this representation then as that, where the ability of the object to serve as a vessel for multiple meanings and our ability for grasping the several meanings cooperate in making these experiences edifying and memorable. The intentional layering we perceive in the world of art reveals as much about us as it does about its objects.[3]

A reference frame provides the terms in which an object of interpretation and its proffered interpretations are intelligible and appropriate. David Novitz provides an example of the frame-relativity of a word's meaning, saying:

> Consider this example: the sound made by uttering the word "bid." When this sound is taken in conjunction with the conventions of Afrikaans that are undoubtedly pertinent to it, the semantic property that emerges in standard contexts is the verb *to pray*. Taken against the conventions of English, however, the semantic property that emerges is *an offer of money*. Importantly, when once we know from the speaker or the context that the proper conventions in terms of which to construe the sound are the conventions of English, it is exclusively true to say that (in a standard context) the word means *an offer of money*, not *to pray*. It follows that it is not as if one is free, when responding to cultural objects, to impose one's own cultural understandings or preferred systems of explanation on the object, no matter how pertinent we take them to be. One is bound by those conventions that actually apply to it. And it is our sometimes hard-won knowledge of these conventions that allows us to say of anyone interpreting the object *ab initio* that their interpretation is either true or false, right or wrong.[4]

A word's meaning is objectively *found* within the terms of a reference frame, not made by single interpreters who "project" meanings. Further, Jitendra Mohanty says:

> Thus the empirical person living in the world, speaking his language, using his conceptual scheme, sharing in his tradition, is subject to a point of view of his own, of his community. But he does not, in his prereflective naivety, know that he sees the world from a standpoint. He lives in, perceives, knows the world, the only world that is there for him. That,

however, he is subject to a perspective, a standpoint, a conceptual framework, is brought out by reflection.[5]

Substituting the word, "work," for my phrase, "object of interpretation," Peter Lamarque suggests that we should understand interpretive activity in terms of a three-tiered scheme: (1) objects, (2) works, and (3) interpretations. More fully, he articulates his scheme in such a way as to allow for multiplist conditions to obtain between interpretations and a *work*. He says:

> My tripartite scheme, for artworks, is between object, work, and inter- pretation. Interpretations apply strictly to works, not to objects per se . . . I believe there could be multiple interpretations of *works*. But I don't think there are interpretations of objects, as such, except in a rather spe- cial sense. . . . I share with [Arthur] Danto the intuition that the existence of an object . . . or a "mere real thing," is never sufficient for the exis- tence of a work.

> It is at the second level that *works* appear; literary, philosophical, his- torical works; paintings, etchings; musical works; sculptures. These are human creations; they depend on human intentions and *cultural condi- tions*. They are intentional objects not only because they owe their ori- gins to intentional acts but also because their identity conditions are partly determined by how they are *taken* or *thought to be* relevant by cultural communities (although not so as to demand any narrowly de- fined singular interpretations). They cease to exist when there is no longer the possibility of their eliciting the appropriate kinds of responses (being identified, being understood, being appreciated, being valued) among suitably qualified respondents. . . . Works are necessarily associ- ated with some object or other . . . but they are not identical with the ob- jects that constitute them. The statue is not identical with the piece of marble, because they have different identity conditions. . . .

> The complex interplay between work and interpretation (noted by [Paul] Thom and [Michael] Krausz)—the way that interpretations seem to be able to shape works, as well as determining modes of interpretation— loses some of its paradoxical nature when set in this framework. How can an *object* change its properties under an interpretation? . . . That is indeed paradoxical. But the answer is that it is not an *object* but a *work* whose properties are affected. It is not obviously paradoxical that work- identity, in some cases, should be partially determined by interpretations placed on the work (where, for example, different features are high- lighted as salient). The to-ing and fro-ing between work-properties and interpretively imputed properties is precisely what is meant by the her- meneutic circle.[6]

I concur with Lamarque's view that "Works . . . are intentional objects . . . they are not numerically identical to their material embodiment . . . and their continued existence depends on the existence of the practices within which they acquire their identity."[7]

Note Lamarque's three tiers of interpretive activity are relative to an iteration. We may bracket the marble of a statue (initially in tier 1) as the "work" (tier 2) of an interpretation (tier 3). The marble of the statue (initially tier 1) might call for an anterior object (an anterior tier) in relation to it—for example, its chemical composition. This open-endedness of an anterior tier 1 suggests that we can never reach any "rock bottom" level at which we can come to a most basic or "Ur" tier. Again, at the top end of the tiers, an initial interpretation (tier 3) may become the work (tier 2) in relation to which a subsequent interpretation (a subsequent tier 3) may be offered. The iterations are indefinitely open-ended in both directions. (See chapter seven.)

In contrast to Lamarque's and my position, Nicholas Maxwell seeks to collapse the distinction between interpretation and object of interpretation (or work). He argues, first, that a work of art *is* its own interpretation. Call this his "reflexive" thesis. Second, he argues that the interpretation that is the work of art is the one and only one admissible interpretation of itself.[8] Notice that even if a work were its own interpretation (whatever that might mean), it does not follow that the interpretation that would be the work is the only admissible one.

But let us focus on Maxwell's reflexivity thesis. By saying that a work is its own interpretation, Maxwell must concede that the work is *about* something. But in answer to the natural question, what is the interpretation about? he must answer, "itself." Yet this answer denies that the interpretation is about something beyond itself. I suggest that for something to be about something, the second must be different from the first. In this respect, interpreting is like explaining in that it takes an object. An explanation is an explanation *of* something. An *explanans* is different from an *explanandum*. An *interpretans* is an interpretation of an *interpretandum*. Maxwell goes so far as to privilege works themselves as "core" interpretations. Other interpretations that *are* about something other than themselves he calls "adjunct" interpretations. Core (or reflexive) interpretations take "pride of place," as Maxwell puts it. He says, "Adjunct interpretations can only be, at most, ad hoc additions to the correct interpretation, the work of art itself."[9]

I agree with Maxwell that—in *some* sense—we ought to give pride of place to the work of art. Critics, historians, and writers are often so preoccupied with interpretations (and interpretations of interpretations) that they lose sight of the work of art. But the refusal by many artists to offer interpretations of their work does not establish that their work is an interpretation of itself. By such refusal to interpret, the artist may just be inviting the viewer to *look* at the painting, to *attend* to it, instead of engaging in interpretive activity at all. But Maxwell misleadingly takes such refusals as grounds for his reflexive thesis which, again, violates the distinction between interpretation and object of interpretation. Giving pride of place to the work of art is no endorsement of Maxwell's thought that the work of art provides the single interpretation of itself.

In turn, on quite different grounds, Cristoph Cox also asserts that the distinction between interpretation and objects of interpretation cannot be sustained. He asserts that the firm distinction between object of interpretation and interpretation breaks down. More fully, he says:

> Interpretation never is or can be a matter of "getting the text right" . . . even the most faithful interpretation will involve something other than simple repetition.
>
> Interpretation always involves transformation—or as [Friedrich] Nietzsche polemically puts it "forcing, adjusting, abbreviating, omitting, padding, inventing, falsifying and whatever else is of the *essence* of interpreting." To put it another way, no interpreter of a text (with the possible exception of the classical musical performer . . .) ever cares to reproduce the original, which, after all, already exists. Instead, he or she cares to bring something new into the world, namely a new text that *transforms* (by selecting, highlighting, rendering in a different medium, etc.) the original text. And I think that this basic fact puts singularism under strain.[10]

Cox is right that interpretation always involves transformation in the assignment of significance. But that something new is always added by interpretive activity does not entail that the initially identified object of interpretation is what is transformed or displaced. It does not entail that in interpretive activity a perpetual changing of the subject occurs. It does not entail that an interpretation cannot be about an identifiable and re-identifiable work at all. It does not entail a perpetual pluralizing that results in indefinitely many singularist cases. The transformation that *is* characteristic of interpretive activity entails no violation of the distinction between interpretation and object of interpretation—a distinction that can be drawn and redrawn upon every iteration of the transformation in question. Cox continues:

> The world is not some independent given thing out there that our job as knowers is to represent adequately. Instead, subject and object, self and world are terms in a symbol system (Nelson Goodman), web (Richard Rorty), text (Jacques Derrida), or discursive field (Michel Foucault). Similarly, in the aesthetic context, the constructionist undermines any firm distinction between interpretation and text. For the constructionist ([Friedrich] Nietzsche or Derrida, for example), the text is always itself an interpretation, a reworking of materials already on hand; and any new interpretation is an interpretation of an interpretation, with no ultimate or

final *Ur*-text underlying this process. On this model, then, the question about interpretation is not the realist question "is it right (in the sense of 'faithful')?" but the pragmatic, constructionist questions "is it interesting?" "is it new?" "is it useful?" "is it important? . . . In short, the artist is an interpreter and the interpreter an artist.[11]

When Cox argues for the deconstruction of the distinction between interpretation and its work or object of interpretation, jazz improvisation motivates his thought. He says: "[T]he 'interpreters' are the authors of new texts."[12] But improvisation does not amount to the deconstruction of the distinction between interpretation and its objects of interpretation. Improvisation *does* result in new works. But that does not undercut the repeated applicability of the distinction between interpretation and its objects of interpretation. Cox rightly rejects:

> any firm distinction between interpretation and text . . . the text is always itself an interpretation, a reworking of materials already on hand; and any new interpretation is an interpretation of an interpretation, with no ultimate or final *Ur*-text underlying this process.[13]

Yet, this is to say that the distinction can be applied and re-applied in different iterations. The interpretation-text may become the object of interpretation of a subsequent interpretation and the preservation of the distinction between interpretation and its objects of interpretation still mandates no offending notion of a final or ultimate Ur-text.

Cox is right to observe that interpretive activity does transform the text via translation, selection, supplementation, and deformation. Interpretation is a constructive project that challenges the firmly drawn distinction between a work and any interpretation at a fixed, invariant place. He rightly challenges a hierarchy that would place interpretation above work. But he exaggerates his claim that the interpreter is an artist in the sense of being one who perpetually re-creates a *work*. For his formulation entails that no interpretation *of any given work* could exist, since the work itself would be constantly changing. Again, we must hold the work relatively fixed for the possibility of interpretive activity at all. *That there might be no "firm" and unchanging distinction between interpretation and work does not mandate that none exists.* Under the force of transformation, we should not reject the possibility of applying and re-applying the distinction between works and interpretations. A *work-transformation*'s existence does not disallow reapplication of the distinction.

The claim that interpretation always involves transformation does not entail that we cannot distinguish between interpretation and its objects of interpretation. Instead, forcing, adjusting, abbreviating, omitting, padding, inventing, and falsifying results in the production of new works or objects of interpretation, which we may, in turn, interpret. Instead of deconstructing the distinction, Cox shows how transformation provides ever-greater possibilities for its application. As persons make new works, they may reapply the distinction.

Five

ON IMPUTATION: AGAINST PROJECTIONISM

1. Imputation

We could say that the identity of an object of interpretation may be determined by an interpretation "put upon" it; an interpretation may project nontrivial properties on to an object of interpretation which then become a part of the object of interpretation. In contrast, I hypothesize that *interpretations* do not project properties on to their objects of interpretations. Instead, we *discover* properties of objects of interpretation in the context of the reference frame(s) in which the objects of interpretation reside. If we must speak of imputation in general terms, let us say that reference frames—not interpretations—impute, without the thought that they impute anything *on to* something separate and preexistent.

Without embracing Nelson Goodman's conclusion, consider his suggestive example:

> A friend of mine was stopped by an officer of the law for driving 56 miles an hour. She argued, "But officer, taking the car ahead of me as fixed, I was not moving at all." "Never mind that," replied the officer. "You were going 56 miles an hour along the road, and (as he stamped his foot) this is what is fixed." "Oh, come now, officer, surely you learned in school that this road as part of the earth is not fixed at all but is rotating eastward on its axis. Since I was driving westward, I was going slower that those cars parked over there." "O.K., lady, I'll give them all tickets for speeding right now—and you get a ticket for parking on the highway.[1]

The dispute between the speeder and the officer concerns which reference frame should be invoked. The driver coaxes the officer to change his reference frame—to change what he takes as fixed—in accord with his interests and purposes. The officer is interested in avoiding mayhem on the roads. At the same time, the driver was not both speeding and not speeding at the same time in the same respects. Instead, she was speeding relative to one reference frame and not speeding relative to another reference frame. (The idea of speeding, as we ordinarily understand it, does not apply according to the astronomical reference frame advanced by the driver.) While we may invoke more than one reference frame in accord with opposing interests and purposes, for some reference frames, once fixed, they mandate a single admissible interpretation. Once the officer's reference frame is fixed (by stamping his foot on the ground), he determines the driver to have been speeding. Within that reference frame, we can arrive at a single right answer to the question whether the driver was speeding. Notice, a conflict of interests and purposes may arise that in turn gives rise to a conflict about which reference frame we *should* adopt. In order to avoid getting a ticket, the driver implicates an astronomical reference frame. She has interests and purposes different from those of the police officer.

Good reasons for choosing one reference frame over another may be offered in relation to designated interests and purposes. The multiplicity of admissible reference frames does not entail that several interpretations, within a given reference frame, are admissible. The multiplicity of admissible reference frames is compatible with there being one or several admissible interpretations in a given reference frame.

But can a given object of interpretation embedded in one reference frame be the same if it is also embedded in another reference frame? Must interpretive activity across reference frames change the identity of that which is interpreted? I will return to these questions in chapter seven.

2. Projectionism

How objects of interpretation or works might "take on" properties by virtue of some one's projecting them is altogether mysterious. Instead, properties are objectively discovered in relation to an embedding reference frame. Accordingly, to say that we may impute properties to a given object of interpretation is misleading if to "impute" means to "project." Joseph Margolis says:

> There is no reason why, granting that criticism proceeds in an orderly way, practices cannot be sustained in which aesthetic designs are rigorously *imputed* to particular works when they cannot be determinately *found* in them. Also, if they may be *imputed rather than found*, there is no reason why incompatible designs cannot be jointly defended.[2]

If, by imputation, Margolis means projection, we should jettison the concept, for it invites an unwelcome arbitrariness or subjectivism. We should instead understand the constitution of objects of interpretation not in terms of projection but in terms of reference-frame embeddedness. Objects of interpretation are found, not projected, by virtue of their embeddedness in reference frames. Objects of interpretation are, in truth, what and the way they are in relation to such reference frames.

Yet whether Lamarque embraces a projectionist view is difficult to determine. He does not unpack key phrases that would tell us. He asks:

> How can an object change its properties under an interpretation . . . ?
> That is indeed paradoxical. But . . . it is not an object but a work whose
> properties are affected. It is not obviously paradoxical that work-
> identity, in some cases, should be partially determined by *interpretations
> placed on the work. . . .*[3]

If Lamarque were to understand his phrase, "interpretations placed on
the work" in a projectionist way, it would invite arbitrariness or subjectivism.
We must avoid the implied idea that "my interpreting it so makes it so." His
phrase, "placed on," resembles Joseph Margolis' phrase, "imputed to," which
we might also understand in a projectionist way. Margolis says:

> We cannot even characterize an artwork as such without reference to
> some *interpretation* by means of which its very structure *as* an artwork
> may be exhibited . . . the properties or features that interpretations im-
> pute or ascribe to artworks cannot be construed as the native, *describ-
> able* properties or features of such works.[4]

I agree that while we cannot characterize an artwork as such without reference to *something*, we should not so characterize it in reference to *an interpretation*, but in relation to a reference frame. How *interpretations* could
project properties on to objects of interpretation is mysterious. If some sort of
interpretive activity may alter the identity of an object of interpretation, it
would not be by an *interpretation* being "placed upon the work." Further, if
for any interpretation, a numerically distinct object of interpretation were to
result, only a one-to-one relation between *any* interpretation and the object of
interpretation that it projects could obtain. Accordingly, a multiplist would
have to reject such a *global* projectionism.

3. Frame-Relativity

But another sense of imputation exists, which is not mysterious: that of frame-
relativity. Chhanda Gupta provides a useful basis for its articulation. She
takes a non-cultural example as characteristic of predication in general. Gupta
agrees that interpretations per se can project no properties. In contrast, she
holds that real properties may be instantiated by virtue of their place within
the practices in which they are nested. Gupta invites us to consider the property of the warmth of a hand. Suppose someone touches someone else's hand
and notices that the second person's hand is warm. The first person's hand
does not thereby *make* the second person's hand warm. (That occurring would
be coincidental to the case.) Instead, the second person's hand is warm *in
relation* to the first person's hand. Gupta affirms that warmth is both real and
relational. She generalizes this finding for all real properties:

Surely there is no sense in saying that an object itself is warm apart from the touching hand . . . the object *really* has the warmth, though *relationally and* . . . this feature is not a projection. The object may certainly have a subvisible structure and causal power, but this does not mean that it does not have warmth. *All* features, primary and secondary, are *relational*, but *not unreal* for being relational. . . . When a thing is believed to have some property, even a microstructural property, no realist, and also no internal realist, would say that this was a projection of the knowing mind or of a certain theory the knowing mind conceives *at a certain stage of inquiry*. The knowing mind or the theory it conceives does not *impart* the microstructural property to a stuff any more than the touching hand *imparts* warmth to a body that does not have it.[5]

Gupta holds that warmth is a real property of a hand by virtue of the relation between it and another hand. Warmth is not a real property independent of its relation to another hand or, we might add, to some analogue of it. She continues:

When it was discovered for instance that water is H_2O, no realist would say that the chemical composition was a *projection* of the knowing mind or of a certain theory which the mind conceives at a certain stage of inquiry. The theory does not impose the property of having this chemical composition to a stuff which in reality is something very different. The stuff *really has* the composition which the theory conceives it to have, just as a body really has the warmth the touching hand feels it to have. This claim to be intelligently made however, must involve a reference to *us*—our perceptions, beliefs, conceptions and theories . . . or else severing all relations with us, with our ways of viewing or conceiving it, will make it collapse into something that is wholly transcendent—"secret"— something which is "we know not what."[6]

Consider how Gupta's relationist view might apply to a case in geometry. Euclidean geometry holds that the shortest distance between two points *is* a straight line. Yet Euclidean geometry does not *project* that property onto some *thing*. Correspondingly, in Reimannian geometry the shortest distance between two points *is* an arc. Reimannian geometry does not project that property on to some other thing. Yet, independently of these geometries, we cannot make sense of the claim that the shortest distance between two points is *either* a straight line *or* an arc.

I apply Gupta's relationist view to the property of salience or significance. Accordingly, I affirm that when properties of a work are rightly said to be salient or significant—so characteristic of interpretive activity in general—they are so in relation to a reference frame. These properties are discovered or found, not *made* to be so by projection. Individual interpretations do not project salient properties. They do not "place" anything upon objects of interpretation. Salience or significance is relationally objective in the context of pertinent reference frames.

Here are further cases of frame-relativity in the cultural realm. In *Rightness and Reasons*, I adduced the example of Lucas Samaras's *Head Transformation*, comprised of a set of twelve images of a face, nearly all features of which are variable as between the images.[7] But one variable is held invariant among them, namely, the face's eye (to the viewer's left). When viewers regard the images as a series, the invariant eye is salient by virtue of its invariance in relation to the other images. Yet, when viewers regard the images separately, the invariant eye is not salient. The difference between viewing the image in the context of the series and viewing it alone is a difference in reference frames. In the reference frame of the series, the invariant eye is *objectively* salient. In the reference frame of its autonomous viewing, it is objectively not salient.

Here is another example of salience in relation to a reference frame. Consider Chuck Close's silk screen series, *John*.[8] This work is comprised of ten separate, large, silkscreen prints or "states," progressing from the faintest image in yellow in State 1, to an intense polychromatic fully realized image of *John* in State 10. With each state, Close adds a fuller range of colors, finally to achieve the last state. We can view each image individually as a single "final" product. This way of seeing it is encouraged because Close signed each state print, much as an artist would sign any finished work. At the same time, as the subtitle of Close's show at the Metropolitan Museum—"Process and Collaboration"—suggests, we can construe all but the tenth state as a *technical preparation* for the final tenth state. Whether we see the works individually, or in series, amounts to seeing in distinct reference frames.

Close indicates his preoccupation with switching between the reference frames when he says, "I'm as interested in the disposition of marks on a flat surface . . . as I am with the thing that ultimately gets depicted . . . [It's] shifting from one to the other that really interests me."[9] More fully, State 2, for example, is striking for its colors, bright orange with pale yellow and some cobalt blue and green bits. Within its own terms as a single work, its largely geometrical abstract shapes suggest something like an architectural plan or a city plan perhaps in a Japanese style. If we regard State 2 alone and not as part of the series, the faint cobalt bluish "dots" in the central area present themselves with no special significance. But when State 2 is viewed as part of the series, as *preparatory for* State 10, as *documentary* for such preparation, the reference frame changes. The orange triangular shapes of State 2 recede. In State 10, they become incorporated as subtle hues in an over-all area of dark blue and take on a different character. Further, those initially faint cobalt dots in State 2 come to be seen as *anticipating* the eventual strong eyes in State 10. Insofar as the eyes are salient or significant in State 10, the faint dots in State 2 come to be seen as salient. I suggest that such a shifting amounts to a shifting between reference frames. Salience here is discovered, not a matter of someone's or some interpretation's projecting anything on to anything else. The salience of properties is found in relation to a reference frame. I emphasize found, for it is in relation to some operative reference frame that the designated properties are objectively salient. As indicated by Close's remarks, intriguing switches of frames may exist, where the relations between saliences that arise in different reference frames might "reverberate."[10]

4. The Idea of Reference Frames

I turn now to consider a doubt about the idea of a reference frame. For example, Karl Popper's classic article, "The Myth of the Framework," might suggest to some that, on his view, the idea of a framework is mythic. But this conclusion would be to misread Popper. He is critical not of the idea of a framework per se, but of the often associated claim that frameworks are *incomparable*. He asserts that frameworks can always be compared:

> Note that two logically incompatible theories will be, in general, "commensurable." *Incommensurability* is intended to be much more radical than incompatibility: while incompatibility is a logical relation and thus appeals to one logical framework, incommensurability suggests the non-existence of a common logical framework.[11]

I emphasize Popper's point. Incompatibility assumes one logical framework, while incommensurability assumes the non-existence of a common logical framework. Yet incommensurability may still allow comparability. He continues:

> For example, Ptolemy's astronomy is far from incommensurable with that of Aristarchus and Copernicus. No doubt, the Copernican system allows us to see the world in a totally different way; no doubt there is, psychologically, a *Gestalt* switch, as [Thomas] Kuhn calls it. This is psychologically very important. But we *can* compare the two systems logically. In fact, it was one of Copernicus's main arguments that all astronomical observations which can be fitted into a geocentric system can, by a simple translation method, always be fitted into a heliocentric one. There is no doubt all the difference in the world between these two views of the universe, and the magnitude of the gulf between the two views may well make us tremble. But there is no difficulty in comparing them. . . . I assert that this kind of caparison between systems is always possible. Theories which offer solutions of the same or closely related problems are as a rule comparable, I assert, and discussions between

them are always possible and fruitful; and not only are they possible, but they actually take place.[12]

Yet Donald Davidson argues for the incoherence of a cognate of the idea of a framework or a reference frame, namely, the idea of a conceptual scheme. So let us turn to consider his arguments in the next chapter.

Six

RELATIVISM AND ITS REFERENCE FRAMES

The idea of a reference frame is a cognate of the idea of a conceptual scheme. As such, the idea of a reference frame could be vulnerable to Donald Davidson's critique of the idea of a conceptual scheme. He concludes that the idea of a conceptual scheme is incoherent. But is he correct? If he is correct, is the idea of a reference frame also incoherent?

The context of Davidson's critique concerns his broader attack on relativism. He offers two sorts of arguments against relativism as standardly understood.[1] One sort, with which I agree, opposes the dualism between scheme and content. The other sort, with which I disagree, opposes the coherence of the idea of a conceptual scheme. I will suggest that the notion of a conceptual scheme *is* coherent and that persons of one scheme may understand persons of another. Yet relativism need not assume the offending dualism between scheme and content. A relativist need not, though characteristically does, fall into the trap of assuming the offending dualism.

Relativism standardly holds that cognitive or value claims involving truth or rightness (or their cognates) are relative to the conceptual schemes in which they appear. Such schemes may include reference frames, cultures, societies, civilizations, traditions, historical epochs, points of view, perspectives, standpoints, world views, paradigms, forms of life, practices, languages, linguistic frameworks, networks of categories, modes of discourse, systems of thought, disciplinary matrices, constellations of absolute presuppositions, or symbol systems. Accordingly, the truth of a proposition or the rightness of a way is said to be relative to one or another of such schemes.

1. Preliminary Remarks about Relativism

Before considering Davidson's arguments, here are twelve preliminary points:

(1) Schemes and their cognates are adumbrant in the sense that they have no determinate boundary conditions; they are open; they are indeterminate or indistinct as to their limits. Where, for example, do the Inuit and Canadian cultures begin and end? Where do the Mexican and American cultures begin and end? Where do the Medieval, Renaissance and Baroque periods begin and end? Where do Marxist and feminist perspectives begin and end? For one who holds that truth or rightness is relative to these, it is difficult to specify precisely in relation to *what* such relativizing should operate.

(2) In the above characterization of relativism, I used the word "standardly" to signal that some definitions of relativism do not invoke schemes as defining features. For example, Joseph Margolis defines his non-standard "robust relativism" in terms of:

> two essential doctrines: (1) that, in formal terms, truth values logically weaker than bipolar value (true or false) may be admitted to govern otherwise coherent forms of inquiry and constative acts, and (2) that substantively, not merely for evidentiary or epistemic reasons, certain sectors of the real world open to constative inquiry may be shown to support only such weaker truth-values. That is all.[2]

(3) The recognition of historical or cultural diversity often motivates relativism. Yet that recognition does not amount to relativism, since cultural or historical diversity is logically compatible with either relativism or anti-relativism. An anti-relativist might react to the diversity of beliefs or practices by employing the notion of progress, according to which pertinent beliefs and practices, which differ from our own are thought to be unenlightened or backward. Such an anti-relativist might assume that our views are or should be the end product of a process toward a non-relative truth. True, other people whose beliefs and practices differ from ours might reach a similar conclusion about our beliefs and ways. What the anti-relativist demands is a non-relative criterion applicable to everyone. It would reveal truth and rightness as such.

But the relativist holds that no such criterion exists. Any would-be neutral criterion would reflect the biases or prejudices of our home scheme. Accordingly, to say that some belief or practice is true or right relative to a scheme is to say more than that individual who embraces it happens to believe something, or happens to live according to designated practices. Relativism of truth or rightness is not just an ascription of a belief or an anthropological fact.

The relativist holds that at the boundaries of schemes, where standards of evaluation give out, we have no way to adjudicate between contending claims. We have no context-neutral, objective way to appeal to a putative overarching nature, human nature, absolute principle, or the like. Yet the relativist does claim to have resources necessary to discriminate between distributive claims that fall within a pertinent scheme. The relativist has the resources to say, for example, that it is true that this sentence is composed on a computer, without recourse to extra-scheme considerations.

(4) Anti-relativism does not entail absolutism, the view that a permanent or eternal foundation of meaningfulness, existence, truth or rightness exists. A person may be an anti-relativist but not an absolutist. We may oppose relativism and remain agnostic or even deny absolutism. Davidson, for example, rejects relativism, but that does not commit him to absolutism.

(5) Relativism is not skepticism. The skeptic holds that knowledge about matters of fact or value is impossible. Unlike skepticism, relativism affirms

that such knowledge is possible, yet relative to a pertinent scheme. The relativist sees the skeptic as setting up an impossible goal—absolute truth—and then damning attainable relative truth because absolute truth is impossible, as if an explorer, on a fruitless quest for a mythical treasure, were to toss aside the "lesser" treasures that he or she might acquire along the way. In contrast to the skeptic, the relativist holds that truth or rightness is attainable, even if it is not the absolute truth first desired by the skeptic.

(6) Sometimes, relativism is confused with fallibilism. Fallibilism is the view that, at any stage of inquiry, a person may hold false beliefs. It serves as a tonic for those who might hold that truth is absolute and that they have in fact attained it. But a person could be a fallibilist and still endorse an absolutist notion of truth, as Karl Popper does. He says:

> A . . . doctrine of absolute truth, in fact a fallibilist doctrine . . . asserts that mistakes we make can be absolute mistakes, in the sense that our theories can be absolutely false, that they can fall short of the truth. Thus the notion of truth, and that of falling short of the truth, can represent absolute standards for the fallibilist.[3]

We could embrace the thought that truth or rightness is not relative to schemes, but that at any stage persons could be wrong about their beliefs or ways. Relativism has no special claim on fallibilism.

(7) An absolutist might worry that if no absolute truth to be discovered exists, then no worthwhile goal of inquiry exists. If we cannot aim for an absolute truth, for what can we aim? If no absolute truth exists for everyone, how can we ever say beliefs or practices are true or right? The absolutist worries that by ruling out absolute truth, we rule out the possibility of progress in knowledge. The relativist replies that we have no reason to assume a global view of progress. Knowledge *can* be progressive, if only in a local way according to standards linked to designated schemes.

(8) Relativism is characteristically defined as the view that, in the absence of overarching standards of adjudication between pertinent schemes, such standards are *equally* admissible. I have distinguished such a view from "multiplism" whereby, in the absence of such standards, not all admissible schemes or interpretations are equally preferable.[4] The multiplist claim that several opposing interpretations may be admissible does not preclude our giving good reasons for preferring one interpretation over others. Often no univocal commensurating standards between admissible interpretations exists. I call cases in which no such standards exist "inconclusive." Inconclusiveness does not entail arbitrariness. Instead, it allows for critical comparability and reasoned preferability of admissible interpretations.

(9) Relativism is sometimes understood to entail that mutual *understanding* between those of different schemes is impossible. But relativists need make no such assumption. As Alasdair MacIntyre says, we are not "con-

demned to or imprisoned within our own particular standpoint."[5] Popper concurs when he says:

> Frameworks, like languages, may be barriers; but a foreign framework, just like a foreign language, is no absolute barrier. And just as breaking through a language barrier is difficult but very much worth our while . . . so it is with breaking through the barrier of a framework."[6]

Popper affirms that untranslatability between two languages can be transcended when he says further:

> In the comparative study of these languages we use, as a rule, our own language as a metalanguage . . . in a critical way, as a set of rules and usages which may be somewhat narrow since they are unable completely to capture, or to describe, the kinds of entities which the other languages assume to exist. But this description of the limitations of English as an object language is carried out in English as a metalanguage. Thus we are forced, by this comparative study, to transcend precisely those limitations which we are studying. And the interesting point is that we succeed in this.[7]

(10) Self-referential arguments against relativism are well known. They concern the issue of how we should answer the question whether the thesis of relativism itself is true or right. If we say the thesis is absolutely true, a contradiction results. If we say it is relatively true, its reach is limited to the scheme in which it appears. The second of these alternatives is not vicious if we allow that the relativist's purpose in arguing need not be to convince the non-relativist. The relativist may use arguments or reasons, ampliative reasons, to present his or her view, only to better articulate the view. That is all.

(11) If Davidson's argument against conceptual schemes is sound, it unseats those standard forms of relativism that hold cognitive or value claims are relative to schemes. His argument associates schemes with languages in this way:

> We may accept the doctrine that associates having a language with having a conceptual scheme. The relation may be supposed to be this: if conceptual schemes differ, so do languages. But speakers of different languages may share a conceptual scheme provided there is a way of translating one language into the other. Studying the criteria of translation is therefore a way of focusing on criteria of identity for conceptual schemes.[8]

(12) Let us consider two possible examples of pairs of schemes. I say these are possible examples because, should Davidson's argument be sound,

they would be disqualified as *bona fide* examples. Consider first shame and guilt cultures. Ruth Benedict reports:

> True shame cultures rely on external sanctions for good behavior, not, as true guilt cultures do, on an internalized conviction of sin. Shame is a reaction to other people's criticism. A man is shamed either by being openly ridiculed and rejected or by fantasizing to himself that he has been made ridiculous. In either case it is a potential sanction. But it requires an audience or at least a man's fantasy of an audience. Guilt does not. In a nation where honor means living up to one's own picture of oneself, a man may suffer from guilt though no man knows of his misdeed and a man's feeling of guilt may actually be relieved by confessing his sin.[9]

Notice that in Benedict's characterization nothing precludes a person of the Japanese shame culture from understanding a person of the North American guilt culture. As a "bi-cultural" or "bi-lingual" anthropologist acquainted with Japanese shame culture and American guilt culture, Benedict succeeds in comparing and contrasting them. A person of one culture can understand a person of another. Yet no non-relative standard according to which one culture is right and the other is wrong exists.

Here is a second possible example of a pair of schemes: Indo-European languages and the Hopi language as understood by Benjamin Lee Whorf. He reports:

> We are constantly reading into nature fictional acting entities, because our verbs must have substantives in front of them. We have to say "It flashed" or "A light flashed, " setting up an actor, "it" or "light, " to perform what we call an action, "to flash." Yet the flashing and the light are one and the same. . . . Hopi can and does have verbs without subjects, a fact which may give that tongue potentialities, probably never to be developed, as a logical system of understanding some aspects of the universe. Undoubtedly, modern science, strongly reflecting western Indo-European tongues, often does as we all do, sees actions and forces where it sometimes might be better to see states. . . . This is the trouble with schemes like Basic English, in which an eviscerated British English . . . is to be fobbed off on an unsuspecting world as the substance of Pure reason itself.[10]

As in Benedict, nothing in Whorf's characterization precludes an Indo-European from understanding a Hopi, and vice versa. Nothing precludes mutual understanding. Benedict and Whorf compare and contrast their pairs of examples from the standpoint of a guilt culture in English. Each makes sense of the scheme alternative to hers or his. This does not mean, however, that the schemes are intertranslatable.

2. Davidson's Argument against the
Dualism between Scheme and Content

Let us now turn our attention to Davidson's argument against the dualism between scheme and content. With Davidson, I reject the dualism. He says:

> Conceptual schemes, we are told, are ways of organizing experience; they are systems of categories that give form to the data of sensation; they are points of view from which individuals, cultures, or periods survey the passing scene.[11]

Davidson objects to the idea that data of sensation is *there* (or some analogue thereof) to be organized. Accordingly he rehearses the dualism:

> The idea is then that something is a language, and associated with a conceptual scheme, whether we can translate it or not, if it stands in a certain relation (predicting, organizing, facing or fitting) to experience (nature, reality, sensory promptings). The problem is to say what the relation is, and to be clear about the entities related.[12]

He continues:

> The images and metaphors fall into two main groups: conceptual schemes (languages) either *organize* something, or they *fit* it (as in "he warps his scientific heritage to fit his . . . sensory promptings." The first group contains also *systematize, divide up* (the stream of experience); further examples of the second group are *predict, account for, face* (the tribunal of experience). As for the entities that get organized, or which the scheme must fit, I think again we may detect two main ideas: either it is reality (the universe, the world, nature), or it is experience (the passing show, surface irritations, sensory promptings, sense data, the given).[13]

John McDowell formulates the offending dualism between scheme and content in this way:

> Scheme-content dualism is incoherent, because it combines the conviction that world views are rationally answerable to experience—the core thesis of empiricism—with a conception of experience that makes it incapable of passing verdicts, because it removes the deliverances of the senses from the domain of the conceptual. According to the dualism, experience both must and cannot serve as a tribunal.[14]

Davidson links relativism with the offending dualism between scheme and content. But relativism need not be defined in this way. We need not understand schemes as "organizing experience" or as giving form "to the data of sensation." Instead, we can understand schemes as matrixes in terms of which experience and data are to be understood—without assigning them a status preexisting the schemes in question. Accordingly, no fact of the matter beyond language (as in the Indo-European and Hopi case) would be presumed and no fact of the matter about moral behavior (as in the shame and guilt cultural cases) would be presumed. Some relativists might link their relativism with the offending dualism. But they need not.

As Davidson says, we must reject the dualism. Yet if we do reject the dualism we do not forfeit objectivity. Davidson rightly says:

> In giving up dependence on the concept of an uninterpreted reality, something outside all schemes and science, we do not relinquish the notion of objective truth—quite the contrary. . . . In giving up the dualism of scheme and world, we do not give up the world, but reestablish unmediated touch with the familiar objects whose antics make our sentences and opinions true or false.[15]

Again, versions of relativism to which Davidson's critique of the scheme-content duality are vulnerable are those which assume the duality between what is given to the mind through sensation on the one hand, and concepts which the mind uses to *organize* this given on the other hand. Davidson objects to the thought that an external reality exists *on to which the relativist (or the absolutist) grafts schemes*. The point is not whether *one or more* schemes to be grafted onto such a reality exists—as the traditional standoff between relativists and absolutists presents itself—but whether the idea of *grafting* is wrong headed to start with. Davidson says, "Even those thinkers who are certain there is only one conceptual scheme are in the sway of the scheme concept; even monotheists have religion."[16] Davidson opposes those relativisms *and* absolutisms which presume conceptual schemes taken to "mirror" the world(s). He says further:

> It would be . . . wrong to announce the glorious news that all mankind— all speakers of language, at least—share a common scheme and ontology. For if we cannot intelligibly say that schemes are different, neither can we intelligibly say that they are one.[17]

Davidson's argument against the scheme-content dualism applies to relativism and absolutism if both presuppose that the nature of things independent of schemes exists which "answer to," or are "represented by" pertinent schemes. If we rejected the scheme-content dualism, then the question of relativism versus absolutism, as standardly posed, would not arise in the first place. Yet, since the idea of a conceptual scheme *need not* assume the scheme-content dualism, relativism without the dualism may still deploy the idea of a conceptual scheme. Rejecting the scheme-content dualism does not undercut all relativisms, only those relativisms that assume it. The resulting kind of relativism would be benign, if heterodox, from Davidson's light.

Let us contrast the kind of relativism that assumes the offending scheme-content dualism with the more benign kind of relativism that does not. Consider again the cases of Benedict and Whorf. Recall that Benedict reports, "[t]rue shame cultures rely on external sanctions for good behavior, not, as true guilt cultures do, on an internalized conviction of sin." A person who links relativism with the scheme-content dualism would construe Benedict's example this way. Good behavior denotes a fact of the matter, a phenomenon that is *there* antecedently waiting to be captured, accounted for, or "faced." Shame cultures do this in terms of external sanctions, and guilt cultures do it in terms of internalized convictions of sin. In both cases, good behavior is presumed to be pre-existently constituted before interpretive activity. In contrast, persons who do not link relativism with the scheme-content dualism would drop the pretense of such pre-existence and would instead do what Benedict actually does, namely, speak of good behavior in terms given by the schemes of shame and guilt cultures. Good behavior would be just what is so constituted by pertinent practices in designated cultures, nothing more.

Similarly, consider Whorf's contrast between the Indo-European who, when making sense of action phenomena, reads into nature "fictional acting entities" and the Hopi who does not. A person who links relativism with the offending scheme-content dualism would hold that the nature of action phenomena is pre-existing, constituted before interpretive activity, that the Indo-European and the Hopi both are seeking a "match" between their respective schemes and action phenomena. In contrast, as in Benedict's case, the relativist who does not link her relativism to the offending dualism, would hold that action would be just what is so constituted by pertinent practices in designated cultures. That is all.

An absolutist might concede that the cases that I have adduced—namely, the guilt versus shame cultures and the Hopi versus Indo-European grammars—are conventional. But the absolutist might insist that the scheme-content dualism still applies to such cases as middle-sized objects or to molecules. I agree with Davidson that such an absolutist response is unsustainable because his sound arguments for the rejection of the scheme-content dualism apply globally and not in piecemeal fashion. Contra Davidson, my concern here is to suggest that the idea of a conceptual scheme is coherent as demonstrated in the adduced examples. A more sustained treatment of such entities as middle-sized objects and molecules would follow along lines suggested by Hanna and Harrison as I will discuss in chapter seven.

3. Davidson's Argument against the
Idea of a Conceptual Scheme

Let us turn to Davidson's argument against the idea of a conceptual scheme. He argues that the coherence of the idea of a conceptual scheme requires the coherence of the idea of an *alternative* conceptual scheme. Yet, he argues, the idea of an alternative conceptual scheme is incoherent, for if an alternative conceptual scheme is *translatable* into the first conceptual scheme, it is not "alternative." He says, "the failure of intertranslatability is a necessary condition for difference of conceptual schemes."[18] So, if a putative alternative scheme is not translatable, nothing intelligent can be said about it to distinguish it from the first conceptual scheme. Accordingly, Davidson says, "we could not be in a position to judge that others had concepts or beliefs radically different from our own."[19] Since grounds for distinguishing one conceptual scheme from an alternative scheme do not obtain, the distinction between them collapses. With that collapse, the coherence of the very idea of a conceptual scheme is unseated, as is the coherence of those forms of relativism that presume the coherence of the idea of conceptual schemes. Let us call this Davidson's "alternativity" argument.

Davidson's alternativity argument applies to partial and complete translatability. It applies to portions of a language or a scheme that are non-translatable and to language taken as a whole. If portions or the whole of a language are not translatable they could not be recognized as alternative, and if they are translatable they are not alternative.

According to Davidson, we characteristically make sense of people by listening to what they say and that means that they must speak a language that we understand. If we cannot understand a person's utterances, we could not ascribe beliefs to them. We could not say whether they had a different conceptual scheme. We could not tell whether they are speaking a language in the first place. Accordingly, Davidson advances his principle of charity: namely, we can make sense of what a person means only if we begin by assuming that their beliefs are largely in agreement with our own. Anomalies inevitably arise. We can deal with them in one of two ways. Either (1) we can say a failure of translation occurs and therefore a difference in conceptual scheme obtains, or (2) we can say that a difference in belief exists. But no hard and fast rule exists that forces us to deal with anomalies according to (1) or (2). Therefore, if we come across a putative partial failure of translation, we can always say that it arises from a difference of belief as opposed to a difference of conceptual scheme.

But we must be careful here. Because no hard and fast rule exists in this regard, it does not follow that we can always say that the partial failure of translation is a matter of belief instead of scheme. Further, designating what is "partial" and what is "complete" is difficult. The limits of language are always emerging and open, partial all the way through. What, after all, could count as a complete natural language like Chinese or English?

We might retort to Davidson's alternativity argument that all that it shows is that, while we may have *no criterion to verify* the presence of an alternative scheme, it may still exist. But Davidson might well reply that indicating the possibility of an alternative scheme is not enough. We must also give some reasons or grounds to believe that such an alternativity exists. Yet we can give such reasons or grounds. First, enough overlap exists between those of guilt and shame cultures for its inhabitants to compare and contrast their cultures with one another. Within that conversational space inhabitants may *show* one another their disparities concerning the moral character of what they do or the grammatical character of what they say.

We might be tempted to say that we can distinguish conceptual schemes by taking a neutral stance by divesting ourselves of all schemes and then comparing those that present themselves. But Davidson disqualifies this possibility because conceptual schemes are embedded in languages. To divest ourselves of all schemes would require giving up the use of language. Language is necessary for thought. So, if we give up the use of language, we could not even compare. Davidson says:

> Speaking a language is not a trait a man can lose while retaining the power of thought. So there is no chance that someone can take up a vantage point for comparing conceptual schemes by temporarily shedding his own.[20]

According to Davidson's alternativity argument—which associates translatability with understandability—the two pairs of examples adduced earlier in this chapter, because of their "would-be" intertranslatability, cannot be *bona fide*. Each of the pair is not an alternative to the other. In contrast, I suggest that understanding between people of different schemes is possible despite that there may be no complete translatability between them. Davidson might reply that the examples I offer are not *bona fide* as alternative frameworks, since understanding is possible and therefore translation is possible. Such a reply would disallow that understood schemes can be non-translatable. It would disallow the testimony of bilingual speakers that they understand different languages despite that full translations are not forthcoming. In sum, Davidson holds that nontranslatability is a sufficient condition for non-understandability. But I suggest that a failure of translation does not imply a failure of understandability. Mutual understandability does not entail translatability, although translatability might entail understandability.

MacIntyre observes that translation is not always possible. Yet we can make sense of alternative cultures; we can understand persons of alternative cultures. Translatability is not necessary for understandability. So the non-translatability of schemes does not bar us from saying that one is alternative to the other. Accordingly, even if shame cultures and guilt cultures were not translatable, a person of a guilt culture like Benedict could still understand persons of a shame culture, and, presumably, vice versa.

I return to the question of partial translatability. As David Wong suggests, we can gloss terms of a language even if we have no strict equivalent terms in one's home language. He says:

> When translators of the Chinese word *ren* in the *Analects* render it as "goodness," or "benevolence," or "humanity," or "authoritative personhood" we know these are just approximations. We look at what people say about the role of the concept as one for comprehensive virtue, and we may bring to our understanding of comprehensive virtue, perhaps, our understanding of Greek ethics, but we know that this is also just an approximation. We are told that Confucius at one point associates *ren* with loving persons (*Analects* 12:22), but we should also be careful about equating whatever notions of love we have with the one Confucius was using in this context . . . "Goodness" or "humanity" or "benevolence" or "authoritative personhood" serves more like a pointer.[21]

We should not take the "pointer" of which Wong speaks to point to a determinate equivalent term or phrase. The idea that a determinate equivalent term must exist ignores a characteristic context in which questions of translation arise. When we translate from Chinese to English, a word in a legal document pertaining to the transfer of property, for example, we assume acquaintance with different institutions of property rights. Accordingly, we cannot translate independently of the practices and purposes to which translation is put. The multiplicity of pertinent practices and purposes undermines lexical equivalencies.

Further, an interpreter may have more than one "home" scheme, without full translatability between them. As MacIntyre observes:

> One of the marks of a genuinely adequate knowledge of two quite different languages by one and the same person is that person's ability to discriminate between those parts of each language which are translatable into the other and those which are not. Some degree of partial untranslatability marks the relationship of every language to every other.[22]

Languages not fully translatable between one another need be no barrier to one's understanding them. MacIntyre emphasizes the point:

> *Notice that this recognition of untranslatability never entails an acknowledgment of some necessary limit to understanding.* Conversely, that we can understand completely what is being said in some language other than our own never entails that we can translate what we understand. And it is this ability both to understand and to recognize the par-

tial untranslatability of what is understood . . . [that creates] the pre-
dicament of the bilingual speaker.[23]

By distinguishing between translatability and understandability, MacIntyre claims that we can understand two languages or appropriate portions
thereof while not being able to translate between them. Bilingual speakers
need to be able to do this in order to determine—as he or she does—what is
not translatable from one language to another. Just as untranslatability does
not entail a limit on understanding, understanding does not entail translatability. MacIntyre's point undercuts Davidson's association of untranslatability
with non-understandability. So even if we were to hold fixed non-
translatability as a criterion of conceptual schemes, it would not follow that
we would not be in a position to recognize an *alternative* conceptual scheme
as a *bona fide* case.

Without translatability, we need not remain silent about an alternative
conceptual scheme. The putative "alternative" need not be absorbed into the
home conceptual scheme. We can still distinguish conceptual schemes. Hilary
Putnam agrees when he says:

> If one recognizes that the radical interpreter himself may have more than
> one "home" conceptual scheme, and that "translation practice" may be
> governed by more than one set of constraints, then one sees that concep-
> tual relativity does not disappear when we inquire into the "meanings"
> of the various conceptual alternatives.[24]

In short, mutual understandability does not entail translatability, and translatability is not necessary for understandability.

4. Adumbrance of Conceptual Schemes

Here now are my misgivings about those relativisms tied to conceptual
schemes and their cognates. The difficulty with such relativisms concerns not
the incoherence of conceptual schemes, but their adumbrance. The schemes
relative to which truth or rightness is supposed to operate often cannot be
unambiguously delineated. Where, after all, does a guilt culture and a shame
culture begin and end? Where, after all, does an Indo-European language and
a Hopi language begin and end? For that matter, where do Chinese and English begin and end? The difficulty obtains because in saying that truth or
rightness is relative to such schemes, no ready application procedures exist. If
I say that truth is relative to my scheme, which is my scheme? What if I have
multiple schemes that blend into one another? What if I am a Chinese, American, New Yorker, feminist? My misgiving concerns the *applicability* of the
relativist rubric upon pertinent schemes. That does not mean that such schemes
are incoherent. It only means that a difficulty exists in applying the notion of a

scheme to do the job that relativists standardly demand of it. Schemes are characteristically adumbrant. They may overlap in complicated and unstable ways. The adumbrance of schemes does not, though, disqualify understanding between inhabitants of each.

In sum, I join Davidson in disallowing the scheme-content dualism, and thereby those relativisms which assume it. However, not all relativisms need assume the offending dualism. Further, I allow the coherence of the idea of conceptual schemes and their mutual understandability, dislodging the link between non-translatability and non-understandability. Finally, in face of the characteristic adumbrance of schemes, those relativists who do not assume the offending scheme-content dualism still need to provide procedures under which their relativism can apply.

Insofar as the idea of a reference frame is a cognate of the idea of a conceptual scheme, it, too, is characteristically adumbrant. Yet, as the range of examples adduced in the present volume testifies, such adumbrance does not disqualify their application.

Seven

CONSTRUCTIVE REALISM:
AN ONTOLOGICAL BYWAY

In the context of a theory of interpretation, the need for an ontological account turns out to be contentious. For example, Paul Thom says:

> I see no reason for theorists of interpretation as such to engage in metaphysical issues, of which the existence of transcendental objects is one. The object of interpretation, on my account, is a "further" object only in the sense that the object of interpretation is further removed from the governing concept that is the object-as-represented.[1]

The force of Thom's remark derives from his phrase, "for theorists of interpretation." For Thom, in the context of interpretive activity, the "further object" is not an object as such, and so, on his view, it needs no further accounting. Yet it remains that our understanding of "objects of interpretation" requires an ontological accounting.

Bernard Harrison and Patricia Hanna may agree with Thom's point that objects of interpretation already fall under a "governing concept" as Thom understands it, without making any further commitments about "objects" that might be thought to be independent of all reference frames. Yet such an agreement amounts to an ontological position. While the theory of interpretation may be distinct from an ontology of its objects, they are closely related. We can hardly engage in the first without the second.

1. Ontology and Methodology

I have suggested that we need to secure an object of interpretation as the single object of interpretation that it is, in order for it to answer to a singularist or a multiplist condition. Yet while ontologies may provide accounts of the sort of thing objects of interpretation and interpretations are, they provide no criterial decision procedure for sorting which particular interpretations are admissible and which are not. Neither can ontologies fix whether a given object of interpretation ought to count as one or more. Ontologies provide no grounds for sorting or "triaging" admissible from inadmissible interpretations from the pool of considered interpretations. A realist, a constructivist, and a constructive realist can all agree that horses exist and that unicorns do not exist. They can all agree that William Shakespeare's *Hamlet* is about a Danish, not a Bulgarian, prince. They can all agree that Vincent Van Gogh's *The Potato*

Eaters is not about the attack on the New York City World Trade Center on 11 September 2001 and they can all agree that the Holocaust actually happened. But as ontologies, realism, constructivism, and constructive realism provide no method of separating admissible from inadmissible distributive claims such as those just mentioned. Realists, constructivists, and constructive realists may agree about triaging such distributive claims in the same way, while disagreeing about the *sorts* of things they are.

2. A Mistaken Byway: Metaphysical Realism

David Novitz offers a metaphysical realist ontology when he says:

> It seems plain that I can learn that people desire food or that a motor accident occurred at 5:10 p.m. on 25 June, without believing or inventing a specific story which somehow informs my experience. If I am right there is no good reason for denying the existence of so-called prenarrative facts, or for insisting . . . that all experience and knowledge must be mediated by, or derived from, narrative. Not all explanations are narratives, nor are all theories, descriptions, lists, annals, or chronicles.[2]

By contrast, I agree with Harrison and Hanna that "objects" as such and objects of interpretation are intentionally constituted. They are so by virtue of their embeddedness in some reference frame.

But, with Novitz, Michael McKenna objects. He holds that intentional layering must stop somewhere, with objects such as:

> pterodactyls, crocodiles, stars, and masses of gold. Also, properties like the color red, or being lighter than gold, exist; truths, like the second law of thermodynamics, exist; and so forth.[3]

His realism holds that the world and its objects exists in a determinate way and that there exists only one right interpretation for each of its aspects.[4] According to him, individuals exist, complete with fixed identity conditions. He says:

> Individuals exist. In a description of the ultimate nature of reality, we must make room for the notion of a countable, datable item, a particular, a thing, an entity—one of a possible many. . . . [This] is a thesis that, for current purposes, we can count as axiomatic. Included in what exists are rocks, socks, and seagull flocks. These items fall into different categories. The crucial categories are between those items falling within the domain of natural kinds and those falling within the domain of the artificial. Rocks fall within the camp of natural kinds; socks in the camp of artifacts. Seagull flocks are, likely, a logically complex case involving the natural kind "seagull" and the artificial kind "flock."[5]

The items that he mentions do exist. That is not at issue. What is at issue is whether they constitute the ultimate nature of reality. I hold that—if the very idea of an ultimate nature of reality is coherent at all—it is not populated by such differentiated objects, for such objects are the products of objectifications. They are products of interpretive practices. This holds for the objects he enumerates.

McKenna parcels his realist and constructivist concessions when he says:

> Let the constructivist loose on the artifacts; allow them to loosen identity conditions on works of art, making hay with all kinds of imputed properties and multiply admissible interpretations of *Hamlet* plays, Beatles tunes, or ships owned by characters named Neurath. But the laws of thermodynamics, and the genetic constitution of bunny rabbits and weasels are not up for grabs, are not subject to revision and construction from the conventions constituting our "conceptual schemes" . . . we restrict the range of realist commitments to the domain of the naturally occurring. Let constructivism rule in the realm of human fabrication and convention.[6]

While he holds that natural kinds reflect the ultimate nature of reality I hold that "natural" kinds too are subtended under pertinent reference frames. He says:

> Nature can be carved at the joints. Where the carving does hit the joints, we have no reason to believe that the level of discourse in which the carving is expressed is mere intentional layering. We have intentional layering, but driven by a world found, not one made. . . . If nature presents itself to us with joints that we might carve, and if what it presents will not sway to our conventions, then nature sets the limits; we do not.[7]

Here is where my constructive realism collides with McKenna's metaphysical realism. He says:

> Now we have individuals and kinds. If, at the most primitive level, a metaphysics acknowledging particulars requires a commitment to properties or features, then da stuff [the pre-praxial]comes differentiated. However da stuff is, the world comes framed in kinds, not just in raw gunk out of which kinds get formed.[8]

On the contrary, I affirm that we cannot understand objects as such—whether natural or cultural—independently of reference frames. This is not just an epistemic claim about what we can understand, but an ontic claim about the identities of objects. But to infer from this (as constructivist Nelson Goodman, for example, appears to think) that nothing is *there* is a mistake. To infer that no undifferentiated stuff before the performance of practice exists is mistaken.

McKenna criticizes Goodman's extreme constructivism when he says:

> To say something about anything (including the world), it has to be said. Naturally, said things are said in languages. From these two morsels we are to move to the quite dubious point that no aspect of the world is free of the conventions of a symbol system or a conceptual scheme.[9]

He is right that these "morsels" do not entail Goodman's thoroughgoing constructivism. From Goodman's claim that the way things are is assertable only within a "symbol system," it does not follow that things are in no way independent of such symbol systems or reference frames. But, significantly, from Goodman's conclusion not being entailed, it also does not follow—as McKenna asserts—that *a differentiated way* that things are, independently of symbol systems or reference frames, exists. Nor does it follow what that way is. These matters are left open. In this logical space is where I join Harrison and Hannah's practice-centered account of objects.

McKenna seeks to ground his realist metaphysics in individuals located at the level of an ultimate nature of reality when he says, "we must make room for the notion of a countable, datable item, a particular, a thing, an entity—one of a possible many."[10] He takes it that individuals reside at the ultimate or most primitive level, where reality is taken to be cut at its joints, where kinds reside in their un-analyzable states. But I see no reason to assume that individuals should reside in such an ultimate nature of reality. I resist the temptation to ground individuals there.

Yet we might ask, if we disallow the idea of an ultimate reality—or the idea that such a reality must be constituted by individual objects—what would happen to our ability to negotiate everyday life? What would happen, for example, to our ability to negotiate between automobiles on busy streets? I suggest that we should grant everyday pedestrians' descriptions and those of biologists, botanists, and physicists according to their interests and purposes. In everyday life, we pick out middle-sized objects—such as cars and trucks on busy streets motivated by our intense interest to stay alive, inevitably within reference frames in which the phenomenon of human life applies and is valued. That does not mean, though, that middle-sized objects are inherently more privileged than, say, those of the biologist, botanist, or the physicist.

In contrast to McKenna's sort of metaphysical realism, I affirm a constructive realism according to which we may still speak of "natural" kinds but in a non-essentialist way. Rocks fall under the constructed category of the "natural," and socks fall under the constructed category of the "cultural." Yet the *real* joint between them is a taxonomic achievement. In this way, "made" and "found" are made compatible, keeping in mind that the "made" may be as "real" as the "found." To say that that which is made is not real is wrong. Saying that what is found cannot also have been made is also wrong. No exclusive disjunction between the constructed and the real, or between the made and the found is needed.

McKenna draws a sharp distinction between nature and culture. In piecemeal fashion, he asserts that realism obtains in the natural domain and constructivism obtains in the artifactual or cultural domain. In contrast, I suggest that the distinction between nature and culture does not coincide with the distinction between realism and constructivism. Neither of these distinctions is exclusive and the two distinctions are not coextensive. McKenna notes that natural elements are found in the cultural realm, when he says:

> All artifacts have to have some natural constitutive basis. People perform plays on stages. Music requires acoustic excitations. Novels are realized on some paper. Poems, in conception, came from some thought, some brain. Chairs are made of wood, or other materials. Canvasses are made of something . . . the honored soul and the dumped baby were constituted out of the biological item, infant.[11]

He assumes that constructivism entails multiplism. But it does not. Just as realism does not mandate singularism, constructivism does not mandate multiplism. The cultural realm has no monopoly on multiplist conditions. Neither does the natural or the middle-sized domain have a monopoly on singularist conditions. We can find both singularist and multiplist cases in both the cultural and the natural realms. Multiplism cannot serve as a criterion of the cultural. We should avoid the temptation to offer multiplism as a *demarcation* that separates the cultural from the natural domains.[12]

Further, no ultimate nature of reality needs to be posited, that is, if by ultimate reality one means ultimate *objects* of the world. Notice that this suggestion leaves open the possibility of an indeterminate (pre-objectual) world as opposed to there being no world at all. Once we reject the realism of McKenna (or, as he calls it, "Plain Jane Realism") we need not embrace Goodman's view. Harrison and Hanna, for example, propound a constructive realism (they call it a relative realism) whose world predates the practices which, in turn, institute the kinds and conditions necessary for the identity of objects. In short, objects are not given in the world. It is practices that objectify.

In sum, we should resist the temptation to place nature (in contrast to culture) in the ultimate nature of reality. True, we can find crucial differences between natural and cultural individuals. But these kinds of individuals need not draw their credentials from a putatively privileged ultimate determinate nature of reality. The differences between such kinds of individuals do not constitute a difference in natural kinds that implicate an ultimate determinate nature of reality, complete with independent joints waiting to be discovered.

3. Harrison and Hanna's Constructive Realism

Harrison and Hanna agree with me:

> (1) that realism and constructivism are not exclusive alternatives, but admit combination in several versions of constructive realism; and (2) that neither realism nor constructivism, nor any version of the two, entails either singularism or multiplism.[13]

They also offer an expanded tripartite distinction between world, practices, and sentences. In accord with their tripartite distinction, they take physical objects to post-date, not predate, practices. As objects, they do not exist prior to practices. What then is the "stuff" to which pertinent practices apply? They reply that this stuff is "conceptually undifferentiated" but not "praxially undifferentiated." They state their core thesis this way:

> In a sense, the world prior to the institution of linguistic practices *is* "ineffable," but only in the sense that, as yet, nothing can be said about it. That world is not "ineffable" in the sense of "unknowable," for it is already richly knowable as a realm of outcomes, and its characteristics qua realm of outcomes are precisely what will determine what propositions we will find to be true or false of it when we are sufficiently equipped with linguistic practices to have a use for such notions as propositions, truth, and falsity.[14]

Here is a quibble about Harrison and Hanna's formulation. Instead of speaking of the world as a realm *of* outcomes, they might better have spoken of the world as a realm *for* outcomes. The difference is significant, for the phrase, "realm of outcomes," suggests the thought that the world follows, or is a product of praxial activity. Their view actually holds that the world precedes such activity.

In any event, contra McKenna, we cannot begin an inquiry with a basic description of uninterpreted objects that populate the World, Reality, or Nature. The pre-praxial world is not a world of objects at all, for objects are "takens" within a reference frame. We should resist the temptation to speak of a world in which objects are "givens" as opposed to "takens" within some reference frame. We should resist what Harrison and Hanna describe as the "specular conception." They say:

> According to the specular conception, the logical form of the sentences by means of which we describe reality must mirror the form of the realities those sentences describe.[15]

With them, I affirm that objects of interpretation derive from the way in which its sentences are enmeshed in conventional practices of our devising. Yet that entails no idealism, understood as the claim that the real is the mental. For the relation between referee and referent is not two-way, but three-way. In the following, Harrison and Hanna show how this is possible:

> What makes an object deliver, relative to a given procedure of measurement, the result that it is n inches long, or m microns long, is because it *is* n inches, or m microns, long. No further fact about the world needs to be uncovered, nor would another language, a logically perfect or perspicuous one, be better adapted to plumb those putatively hidden depths than the ordinary languages of linear measurement.

> We do not need another language in which to talk about the real world, because we are already talking about the real world . . . no gap exists between what we truly say concerning the lengths of things and the way they are "in themselves."[16]

Harrison and Hanna's constructive realism understands itself in three, instead of two, terms, so characteristic of metaphysical realism. The constructive element comes through in their following remarks:

> No direct relationship holds between claims (statements, propositions, whatever) and the reality that they concern. We see a pair of relationships, the first between words and some practice, the second between that practice and the realities on which it operates.

> In the present example, such terms as "length," "modulus" take on meaning not from their relationship to any feature of the world that predates the institution of the practice of linear measurement, but from the roles assigned to them within the structure of that practice. The practice of linear measurement in turn relates to reality or the world through the practical operation of measuring techniques of all kinds. With respect to the schema of concepts, including those of length and modulus introduced by the practice of linear measurement, the world as it exists prior to the introduction of that practice, is indeed, in one sense, undifferentiated: conceptually undifferentiated. But that is not to say that the schema of concepts is undifferentiated with respect to the practical techniques and manipulations that connect the practice to that schema. On the contrary, the world as it exists prior to the institution of the practice is replete with the sort of structure that reveals itself to optical, manual, auditory, manipulation. The world is not praxially undifferentiated. We may think of the world relative to practical techniques, including techniques of measurement, as a realm of outcomes.

Such a realm will deliver the same outcome in response to a given manipulation in wholly reliable ways, ways reliable, that is, from observer to observer, given equal accuracy in the conduct of the manipulation in question.[17]

Again, the phrase, "realm of outcomes," is unfortunate, for by itself, it misleadingly suggests that the world follows, not precedes, praxial activity. But their meaning is patent: the world is already richly knowable qua outcome of praxial activity, if not so understood in the specular view. More fully, Harrison and Hanna say:

What the example shows is that we can admit the world to be conceptually unstructured prior to the elaboration of language, while continuing to hold with perfect justice that, on occasion, what we say about the world correctly characterizes it—correctly characterizes, that is, something external to the symbol-system—because of the (preconceptual) praxial structure of the world, the conceptually structured claims that the introduction of appropriate linguistic practices will in due course put us in a position to assert of it will ultimately turn out to be true or false.

Our practices mediate between a conceptually unstructured world and the conceptually structured truths we assert of it. The notion of truth has no bearing on the world prior to the invention of such practices as linear measurement. The whole point of such practices is to equip us with machinery of truth-determination, including yardsticks and other measuring devices, that takes out of our hands the question of which propositions will turn out to be true of what. The notion of objective truth-determination is part and parcel of the notion of truth itself. Both are conjured into existence through the institution of such practices as that of linear measurement.[18]

They conclude:

Whether multiplism or singularism obtains, in short, is a matter having to do, not with ontology, with the nature of objects of interpretation, but with the nature of our linguistic practices and of the techniques of truth-determination with which they equip us.[19]

We have come full circle. In the course of our ontological inquiry, we have come to see that what is primary as regards ideals of interpretation is not the ontological nature of objects of interpretation, but their handling (technique) in praxial situations. According to Harrison and Hanna's constructive realism, objects are products of reference frames. No sharp distinction exists between finding objects of interpretation and fabricating them. Objects of interpretation cannot be free of construction. Such objects as tables, chairs, quarks, gravitational fields, paintings and works of music exist. Yet our interests and purposes enter our descriptions of such objects. Any description of objects is subtended within a reference frame, the choice of which involves our interests and purposes.

Here is a point of nomenclature. I call Harrison and Hanna's view a Constructive Realism instead of a Relative Realism to downplay any implication of a strident relativism that their phrase might imply and to emphasize the affinity of their view with that outlined under the label "constructive realism" in *Limits of Rightness*. It features the construction of objects instead of the world. But in the end, it matters little what we call the view. What matters is the view.

Harrison and Hanna hold that if we do not allow for an undifferentiated pre-praxial world in which there are no objects yet, nothing from which our objects would be constituted would exist. They take natural and cultural objects to post-date, not predate practices. As objects of interpretation, they do not exist prior to practices. At the same time, Harrison says—and this is what still qualifies Harrison still as a card-carrying realist—the world, "is in no sense constituted by the practices, of linear measurement, for instance, through which we gain access to the possibility of describing it in propositional terms."[20]

With Harrison and Hanna, I affirm that objects of interpretation derive from the way in which pertinent sentences are enmeshed in conventional practices of our devising. As Harrison says:

> There is clearly no way, for reasons we have already adduced, in which the meanings of these terms could be explained by ostensively associating the terms with any element of the extralinguistic world.[21]

But now, what of the world upon which our practices apply, and without which our shared constructive realism would be a realism in name only? If we do not allow for even an undifferentiated preconceptual world, nothing to which our practices would apply would exist. Yet, with Harrison and Hanna, I deny any determinate structure of such a world, a structure independent of any determinative practices. This view entails no idealism. Neither does it entail arbitrariness. To say that the world is conceptually undifferentiated is not to say that it does not exist. At the same time, the undifferentiated world can be no candidate for an object of interpretation.

4. Consequences of Constructive Realism

In chapter two, I indicated my reservations about Harrison and Hanna's assertion that a given object of interpretation may simultaneously answer to a singularist and a multiplist condition. Those reservations should not prejudice my agreement with their constructive realism. I now draw out further consequences of our shared ontology.

At one level of description, we may say that a table is a middle-sized object characteristically used on which to write and to support other middle-sized objects like pencils, books, and cups of coffee. But if we inquire into a table's molecular constitution, the sorts of things just said at the middle-sized level no longer apply. Molecules are not hard, nor can they support middle-sized things. No "in principle" rock bottom description of what is before us exists. In accord with selected interests and purposes, we may choose an appropriate level of description. For no single correct description of what is before us exists. What is before us cannot be described irrespective of reference frame. What is before us remains indeterminate before we invoke reference frames.

Again, such a suggestion might prompt astonishment. We might rightly say that persons who do not blindly walk into a heavily trafficked highway know that if they did so, a car would likely hit them. But, as I have indicated, the statement is so within the terms of middle-sized objects—including our physical bodies—to which most persons attach supreme value. We do not blindly walk into heavily trafficked highways because we value our lives. Yet the notion of human life does not apply at the sub-atomic level. Human life and the value attached to it are emergent phenomena at one level of description. That we are intensely interested in that level does not discount that our interest operates at some level. The choice between levels reflects our interests and purposes.

Just as hardness is predicable of tables but not predicable of constituting molecular structures, and just as thirst quenching is predicable of water but not of hydrogen and oxygen, being alive is predicable of human persons but not of constituting electrons. Hardness, thirst-quenching, and being alive are emergent. They are not predicable of microstructures that comprise them.

We might suggest that my constructive realism is a kind of perspectivism. But perspectivism suggests that *one thing* "has" many sides, and that we may view "it" from many perspectives. Yet constructive realism is more radical. For it questions whether we may speak about the fixed identity of that which is before us at all. The notion that "it" might "have" different aspects is held suspect. Analogously, not only might the proverbial blind persons feel different aspects of the same elephant (perspectivism), but also, alternatively they might feel different elephants. No particular level of description exists that *fully* captures the nature of the things. Granted, each framework of knowing is inherently partial. But we have no fully determinate way in which things *are* in relation to which a description might be *thought* to be partial. So, since no such thing as a single way in which things are exists, no level of description which can fully describe or capture their nature can exist.

Finally, to call a thing a table *or* a constellation of sub-atomic particles is not to say that the table is not real, or that the constellation of sub-atomic particles is not real. As Ronald Moore says:

Things as they occur in our lives are charged with an unending array of meanings, associations, ways of comprehending. The world does not sort itself out for us in any simple way. We persistently and habitually mix what we recognize with what we value, and what we value with what we hope. . . . But, on the other hand, the tree is not just anything we please. The tree is not a prayer shawl, my thumb, a logarithm, London, or Sidney Morgenbesser.[22]

Accordingly, for every level of description, a further level is yet to be unearthed. The description of a given entity at a given level cannot exhaust all of "its" possible levels. The number of levels is open. This open-endedness undercuts the possibility of a comprehensive single interpretation of a presumed common object at all possible levels. No complete list of all possible levels can exist. It remains that when we enter into progressively "deeper" levels and we correspondingly re-bracket our objects of interpretation, we *might* or *might not* "pluralize" the object of interpretation depending upon our interests and purposes.

Notice that lower-level constituting phenomena appear to explain higher-level ones. But such explanation can only be partial and approximate if higher-level phenomena are emergent from lower-level phenomena. Fluidity or thirst-quenchingness are properties of water, but they are not properties of hydrogen and oxygen. These elements partially explain features of water. Adducing hydrogen and oxygen does not fully explain fluidity or thirst-quenchingness. But we should not equate the hydrogen and oxygen with the water that they partially explain. Water is emergent with respect to its constituents. But this does not entail that the lower and higher order entities are the same.

When I say, "this is a book" in contrast to a table or a chair, I signal the middle-sized reference frame in which it is considered. Yet the book is constituted by carbon and other elements. Still, the micro-structural constituents that constitute the book are not the same thing as the book. We should not confuse causation with identity.

If an object of interpretation is held common through its levels, but answers to different interpretations at different levels, a multiplist condition could obtain. Yet if the object of interpretation is re-bracketed at each level *without* holding it to be in common between levels, then the multiplicity of descriptions at different levels would not mandate a multiplist condition. Instead, it would issue in a pluralist condition. If they are deemed different, then no multiplist condition would obtain. So, having innumerable levels of description does not by itself entail a multiplist condition.

I emphasize that the absence of an ultimate level of description does not entail that nothing is real. So having no *ultimate* collection of objects does not entail that nothing is real. What appear to be objects cut at their joints, is the work of practices in the context of pertinent reference frames.

Harrison takes issue with Immanuel Kant on this point.[23] According to Harrison, Kant's concern is fundamentally epistemic. Harrison's concern is fundamentally ontic. Kant's "I know not what" is an epistemic claim that we can know nothing independently of concepts. In contrast, Harrison holds that all the time, we do know the brute world as resisting. Yet it is not a conceptually known world. We have a pre-conceptual knowledge of the world, a real world. At the same time, claims of truth and falsity operate only after the application of practices. Not all knowledge is mediated by concepts. The knowledge of what water feels like when we walk into it, and how it sustains the body when swimming, for instance, is not knowledge mediated by concepts in the sense of "concept" which Harrison's arguments seek to elucidate.

Harrison takes issue with Kant's supposal that our access to reality must operate by way of concepts, by way of concepts in the sense with which Harrison is concerned. Kant holds that no such thing as access to a pre-conceptual reality exists, for he takes the term concept to refer to what structures—constitutes—experience. In contrast, for Harrison, concepts have nothing to do with structuring experience. Instead, concepts arc purely linguistic entities whose function is to structure discourse insofar as thought depends on discourse, not experience.

Harrison allows that—with respect to his praxial linguistic sense of concepts—structured experiences are possible for beings who do not yet possess concepts in the pertinent sense. True, we cannot characterize the pre-praxial world in detail without employing concepts in his sense. Yet we can say what makes the pre-praxial world hospitable to our efforts to institute conceptual thought through linguistic practices. The pre-praxial world is systematically and consistently responsive to "sensory-bodily investigation." It is structured in its capability to respond to such sensory-bodily investigation. In contrast to Kant, Harrison holds that we may pre-conceptually encounter the world, through sensory-bodily investigation.

I have indicated that my ontological inquiry into constructive realism is a byway, as regards the overriding theme of this work, closely related to, yet distinct from issues concerning the *limits of interpretation*. I affirm that if a phenomenon is not countable, it can answer to neither singularist nor multiplist conditions and is uninterpretable. In the following chapters of this book, I will pursue this thought as it applies to the self.

Part Two

TRANSFORMATION

Eight

CHANGING REFERENCE FRAMES, CHANGING EMOTIONS

Interpreters sometimes take an active role in framing a situation. This is especially noteworthy in the case of emotions. In this chapter, I explore the relation between an individual's reference frame and the appropriateness of emotions which are thereby warranted. I argue that different reference frames may warrant different emotions; that incongruent reference frames may result in incongruent emotions; that mixed emotions typically mask different reference frames; that we may embrace different reference frames serially; and that a person can change emotions by changing reference frames.

1. Changing Reference Frames: A Personal Account

I begin with a personal account. I began writing an early version of this chapter in October 1995, shortly before I was to conduct some seminars in Germany, at the University of Ulm. I anticipated that visit with trepidation. I harbored lingering anger toward Germans for exterminating members of my family. I experienced fear that Germans might choose to repeat such acts if circumstances permitted. Still, I accepted the invitation from Ulm, prompted by two considerations. First, more than fifty years had passed since the end of World War II and most then present-day Germans were not involved in that War. Second, I was moved by something that the Dalai Lama said to me during a private audience with him in 1992. When discussing his attitude toward the Chinese, the Dalai Lama said of them, "They are my greatest gurus."

I was perplexed. Here was the spiritual and political leader of a people, 1.2 million out of a population of 6 million, who had died as a direct result of the Chinese occupation. Tibetan culture and history was being systematically destroyed by the Chinese. How could this man regard the Chinese as his gurus? The Dalai Lama explained that the Chinese provide the best vehicle for his developing compassion. His attitude toward the Chinese remains an object lesson for me.

Anger and fear are negative emotions. Just as they may destroy those to whom they are directed, they may destroy those who experience them. I have come to think of the Dalai Lama's stance as one that invites a distinctive reference frame of an evoking situation. The Dalai Lama understands Tibet's situation within the context of a general view about negative emotions. His example served me well when I came to dialogue with contemporary Germans about their struggles to overcome their history. My emotional responses to Germans changed. Today I count some Germans as close friends.

I wish here to explore the relation between a person's construal of a situation within a reference frame and the appropriateness of emotions which are thereby warranted. I will leave open the question of what criteria should be established for what an emotion is. Yet I will mention such emotion-like states as anger, fear, compassion, anxiety, relief, gratitude, joy, sadness, pity, appreciation, concern, at-oneness, exhilaration, love, jealousy, care, and concern.

In his classic article on the rationality of emotions, Ronald De Sousa holds that "an emotion is appropriate, if and only if the evoking object or situation warrants the emotion."[1] De Sousa's remark provides a most useful point of departure. First, a truism. Evoking situations are interpreted situations. They are understood or framed in a particular way. So, to ramify De Sousa's opening remark, we may say that an emotion is appropriate if the evoking framed situation warrants the emotion. Such framing results in recognizing that some features are salient or significant. We may say that an emotion is appropriate if the evoking framed situation warrants it. I will concern myself with what warrants emotions based upon received framed situations. We may judge whether a framed situation is reasonably embraced and we can judge whether these emotions are, thereby, warranted. Sometimes we explore these issues with friends and therapists.

I will provide examples of how changing our reference frame of a situation may change our emotions. Here is one. When in India, I had ordered a taxi to take me from McCleodganj—since 1959 the central location of the exiled Tibetan Buddhist community—to Dharamsala, an Indian town about eight miles down a mountainous road. I was near the Institute for Buddhist Dialectics. The occasion was a demonstration in Dharamsala against a recent maltreatment of a Tibetan monk by Chinese authorities. I was well acquainted with the newly installed schedule of fixed rates for taxis from McCleodganj to Dharamsala. When the Indian driver picked me up and as I entered the taxi, I asked what his fare would be. The driver quoted a figure that was about twice the official rate. I became angry and exited the taxi in a huff, sure that he would overcharge me because I was a westerner. All the while, a Buddhist passerby was witnessing this encounter. He approached me and, in hushed tones, he advised me not to be angry. It would do no good, neither for the driver, nor for me. I should detach myself from the situation and move on. He effectively invited me to switch my reference frame so that negative emotions would dissipate. I would accomplish this by recasting my understanding of my self and of the driver. It is all conventional, the Buddhist emphasized. It just is not worth getting that excited about. More than that: the Buddhist understands negative emotions as impediments in the path toward liberation, which involves the dissolution of the ego-self. All of this was built into the Buddhist passerby's invitation to switch my reference frame.

Generally, when persons switch their reference frame, a corresponding change occurs from one warranted emotion to another. As De Sousa says:

> We have all seen a parent punish a lost child when, on finding it, anxiety turned to anger. *In such cases the focus of attention is not changed by the mere change of belief.* . . . But since the facts are now different, new features of the situation become salient to the same attentive set, in turn provoking shifts in the dominant patterns of concern.[2]

Upon finding the lost child, the parent may experience relief and gratitude, and then anger toward the child for not minding previously given instructions. The reference frame shifts so that different features of the case are discovered and taken as salient. The first reference frame would warrant relief and gratitude. The second would warrant anger.

2. Some Models

For analytic purposes, this example suggests a possible model. A person may hold that, for a given reference frame of an emotionally significant kind, one set of congruent emotions exists, which it warrants. In the case just mentioned, the reference frame in which the parent fixes upon the temporarily lost child, the finding of the child warrants the congruent emotions of relief and gratitude. Then, in the separate reference frame in which the parent fixes upon the child's misbehavior, anger is warranted. Let us call this the one-to-one model, where one reference frame warrants one set of congruent emotions.

I take such sets of emotions as joy and delight on the one hand, or anger and frustration on the other hand, as congruent. I take joy and anger, or delight and frustration as incongruent. In the case of mixed emotions, then, I will be concerned with mixed incongruent emotions. De Sousa observes:

> Emotions are not necessarily compatible: hence although there are cases where emotions mix, in varying proportion, we can also expect a class of cases where one Gestalt, one emotion, crowds out another.[3]

De Sousa's remark suggests the interesting case in which emotions are mixed, presumably warranted by the same reference frame. We may call this the one-to-many model, in which a given reference frame warrants multiple incongruous emotions, or as De Sousa says, "incompatible" emotions, though such incompatibility could not amount to contradiction. For example, joy and sadness may be warranted upon the successful completion of a major long-term project (such as writing a book), or upon seeing a dear friend at the funeral of a beloved third person.

According to the one-to-one model, each reference frame of an emotionally relevant kind can warrant only one set of congruent emotions. According to the one-to-many model, one reference frame can warrant a set of more than one mutually incongruent emotions. But, we might ask, by virtue of the resultant incongruent emotions, should we not posit more than one reference frame? In other words, would the one-to-one model not provide a more satisfactory explanation of the incongruent emotions? Perhaps, upon experiencing both joy and sadness, are we not *in sequence* moving from the frame, which focuses upon completion of the work, to the reference frame, which focuses upon the newly experienced absence of work-direction. Might not the mixedness of emotions prompt ambivalence about which reference frame is in play?

Accordingly, we might be tempted to take the one-to-one model as paradigmatic. Again, in the case of the lost then found child, anger "crowds out" relief and gratitude by virtue of a switch in frame. Alternatively, the encounter with a dear friend may warrant joy under a first reference frame, only to have the reference frame switch upon being reminded that the encounter is taking place at the funeral of a beloved third person. But I see no necessity to assign priority to the one-to-one model. I find no reason to think that the movement from relief and gratitude to anger, or the movement from sorrow to joy results from a shift of reference frame.

Consider another example. A colleague of mine was present when I told a close friend the news of my brother's death. Upon hearing this news, my colleague glanced at me for a fleeting moment and abruptly walked away. I was baffled and then angered by what then appeared to be his callous indifference in my moment of grief. But I might have framed the case otherwise. Perhaps my colleague had difficulty dealing with anyone close to death and I should not have taken his abrupt departure as a sign of indifference but of profound discomfort. Perhaps a more appropriate response of mine should have been pity or compassion instead of anger. Upon the present realization of such a possibility, perhaps my response should have been one of remorse for having unfairly or prematurely judging him as I did. Perhaps I should have framed the situation still differently. Perhaps my colleague was being quite sensitive, withdrawing to avoid intrusion into an intimate space during a moment of personal distress. Perhaps my response in turn should have been one of appreciation. As I ponder this possibility in light of my observation of my colleague's behavior in relation to other matters, I remain ambivalent.

My ambivalence may accord with the one-to-one model. In the first case, the reference frame of my colleague's callous indifference warranted my anger. In the second case, the reference frame of my colleague's discomfort warranted my pity or compassion. In the third case, the reference frame of his sensitivity warranted my appreciation. Since, according to the one-to-one model, anger and pity (or compassion or perhaps appreciation) could not be warranted by the same reference frame, I would not know which reference frame to embrace. But perhaps no reason exists to assume that the one-to-one model should reign. Perhaps anger and pity (or compassion and appreciation) would be warranted in relation to a single reference frame. Perhaps we should not hold the one-to-one model to be paradigmatic. Perhaps the one-to-many model has equal claim to admissibility.

Can a given reference frame warrant mixed incongruent emotions? A given reference frame may warrant a given emotion, and in turn, another frame may warrant another emotion, incongruent with the first. That is not controversial. Controversy arises when, in the flow of experience, the incongruent emotions are so closely associated in time, that we assume that those emotions are warranted by the same frame. In the second case, we may try to offer a more fine-grained description of the distinct frames that are embraced. But whether this is the best model for all circumstances is an open question.

The question then arises whether we can simultaneously embrace more than one reference frame. If we could embrace the multiplicity of reference frames simultaneously, we could expect that each simultaneously warrants a set of congruent or incongruent emotions. Or, two frames may serially warrant respective emotions, and they may only appear to operate simultaneously. As shown in the well known Gestalt duck-rabbit illustration, we can adopt one frame after another serially, but not simultaneously. Correspondingly, in the case of the abruptly departing colleague, we can feel anger or pity (or perhaps remorse or appreciation) in sequence, depending upon which frame we adopt.

3. Frames and Narratives

While a plurality of incongruent reference frames may be reasonably adoptable, the question arises whether we should seek a single reference frame for the longer run. If so, we may choose which one by attending to the *larger narrative* in which a reference frame is nested, a narrative that seeks to satisfy a larger or more enduring set of interests and purposes. As in the case of the abruptly departing colleague, we may note whether he exhibits a general pattern of being unfeeling and rude, of insensitivity in like moments, or a pattern of avoidance when in the presence of grieving persons.

Yet some cases may resist closure. For those cases, we may not be able to pick out the single narrative in which to nest the operative reference frame. Judgments about which of competing reference frames to embrace may remain open, and warranted emotions may remain unresolved. For example, we might harbor anger toward a long standing friend for his negligence in not responding to our repeated messages. But in the face of a revised frame, anger might transmute to concern or pity when the frame is redescribed to include the fact that the friend has been facing bankruptcy and is otherwise preoccupied. Contrariwise, the frame may be yet further redescribed to include the observation that the process of bankruptcy does not take years, and that the friend may be using his threatened bankruptcy as an excuse. In such a case, the significance of the threatened bankruptcy recedes. Concern or pity may be "crowded out" (as De Sousa says) by renewed anger, now compounded by resentment. In each case the appropriateness of the emotion is keyed to a revised reference frame within a revised narrative. No closure on the matter may exist—especially when, after receiving assurances from the friend that other pressures were overriding, and silence and inattention should not be taken as disinterest, there follows again a sustained period of silence and inattention. Unresolved emotions may continue for extended periods.

We may seek resolution of our mixed emotions by attending to the broader narrative in terms of which we make ourselves intelligible to ourselves. The broader narrative may well include the recognition of our general dispositions as would encourage one sort of reference frame over another, such as the recognition of our insecurity, undue sensitivity, or quickness to take offense. At a different level, our dispositions may be tied to soteriological predilections.

In the above example, we might ask ourselves such general questions as, is my friend truly a friend? How long should I tolerate such ambiguity before my psychical investment in the matter becomes unreasonable? What does this relationship mean to me? Answers to such questions construct the shape of our lives.

The choice of reference frame(s) in terms of which we might judge whether some emotions are warranted are (usually covertly) tied to the question of what we might call "summing up" considerations. If a person embraces the thought that at the end of life, a single overriding congruent narrative issuing in a single reference frame should arise, then the handling of particular emotional challenges will look quite different from another who looks upon such matters differently. These issues may be expressed in the choice of one's personal mythology.

About resolving conflicting narratives, Louis Mink instructs:

> Events (or more precisely, descriptions of events) are not the raw material out of which narratives are constructed; rather an event is an abstraction from a narrative. An event may take five seconds or five months, but in either case whether it is one event or many depends upon not a definition of "event" but on a particular narrative construction which generates the event's appropriate description. This concept of "event" is not remote from our ordinary responses to stories; in certain stories we can accept even something like the French Revolution as a simple event, because that is the way it is related to characters and plot, while in other stories it may be too complex to describe as a single whole. But if we accept that the description of events is a function of particular narrative structures, we cannot at the same time suppose that the actuality of the past is an untold story. There can in fact be no untold stories at all, just as there can be no unknown knowledge.[4]

For Mink, the resilience of a reference frame is found not in appeals to presumed facts of the matter but in the degree to which it coheres with an entrenched narrative. As he says further:

Insofar as [narratives] make truth-claims about a selected segment of . . . actuality, they must be compatible with and complement other narratives which overlap or are continuous with them. Even if there are different ways of emplotting the same chronicle of events, it remains true that . . . narratives are capable of displacing each other. This happens, for example, when a narrative makes sense of a series of actions by showing them to be decisions reflecting a consistently held policy, where received accounts could only describe them as arbitrary and surprising reactions, or as irrational responses.[5]

When a given frame does not easily cohere with our entrenched narrative, two options are open: change the frame to fit the narrative, or change the narrative to fit the reference frame. When we are pressed to choose between competing narratives we do so, as Mink suggests, according to such values as consistency, simplicity, and we may add interest and purposes.[6] Mink's point is that we do not choose between narratives by appealing to some inaccessible interpretation-free fact of the matter. At the same time, as De Sousa says:

not just anything goes, . . . as those have learned to their regret, who have attempted to "rationalize" their lives in terms of invented scenarios insufficiently rooted in human nature and the facts of life.[7]

De Sousa does not elaborate on his meaning of "human nature" and "facts of life." These are notoriously difficult concepts to secure.[8] Yet, the range of plausible reference frames has limits. In any event, I resist the thought that an *essential* uninterpreted self which responds to a situation exists. My attitude toward the idea of an essentialist individual self is well expressed by Bronwyn Davies and Rom Harré's anti-essentialist narratist alternative when they say:

An individual emerges through the processes of social interaction, not as a relatively fixed end product but as one who is constituted and reconstituted through the various discursive practices in which they participate. Accordingly, who one is is always an open question with a shifting answer depending upon the positions made available within one's own and others' discursive practices and within those practices, the stories through which we make sense of our and others' lives. Stories are located within a number of different discourses, and thus vary dramatically in terms of the language used, the concepts, issues, and moral judgments made relevant and the subject positions made available within them.[9]

Characteristically we do discuss whether one or another reference frame is more reasonable than another. In therapeutic moments, with the aid of a friend or therapist, we construct or reconstruct reasonable frames which will show that our emotions are or are not warranted.

4. Denying Reference Frames

I have said that when settling upon which reference frame to embrace we may encounter a case that does not easily cohere with our entrenched narrative. We may actually *deny* some reference frames because they do not fit well into a narrative of a particular kind. Here is an account of an instance of my own. Initially I experienced an un-duality, an at-oneness, followed by joy and exhilaration. In turn, these were followed by fear:

> In the spring of 1964, I was walking alone at the foot of Mount Vesuvius and unexpectedly came upon a grouping of bushes, greenery, and flowers in which were a sheep and several lambs. It was a most beautiful sight. I was overcome by a religious feeling. I experienced a connectedness with the environment that was both exhilarating and frightening. Given my intellectual commitments at the time (I was a student of analytic philosophy), I was unable to make sense of this kind of experience. I cut the experience short, choosing not to be present for it. My rational faculties were summoned, and questions began to be put, doubts felt; the moment passed. Later I even chastised myself for permitting myself to experience such a "silly" thing.[10]

Fear of the narrative which I thought was mandated by such an experience crowded out joy and exhilaration. But I now see that such fear was needless. I was mistaken to think that such an experience mandates a traditionally religious narrative, which contradicts rationality. This sort of case appears most naturally to be understood in terms of the one-to-many model: a situation framed in one way warrants joy and fear. Alternatively, we may understand it in terms of the one-to-one model. I could affirm that the experience of non-duality warrants joy, and that its subsequent placement in the (contentiously) assumed narrative warrants fear. The second would "crowd out" the first and experientially falsify the experience of non-duality.

5. Encouraging Reference Frames

The following account of a related experience issued in a vocational commitment:

> Though I have long been exposed to the visual arts, I was not particularly visually sensitive until 1971 at the age of 28. While visiting the studio of a friend and being surrounded by her large canvasses, I experienced myself inhabiting the space visually depicted in them. It corresponded to and somehow forged an "inner" space with which I some-

how felt familiar. It was a space in which I was to journey. I suddenly became visually much more highly sensitive, and, as a consequence, needed to paint—to pursue the journey—and became a painter. Since that time I have experienced the world differently.[11]

I felt an at-homeness, an at-oneness, a "non-duality" in the space depicted in the large canvasses of my friend. To encourage the continuation of such states I pursued an artistic program which, by now, answers to a complex narrative. Since 1971, I have had twenty one-person and eleven two-person art exhibitions in the United States, England, Scotland, and India.

6. Programs for Emotions

Sometimes, as suggested in my earlier example of the Buddhist passerby, warranted emotions may transfigure by virtue of reframing a situation. Such reframing may be motivated by a larger program that concerns the emotions quite generally. In the example of the Buddhist passerby, a general view about positive and negative emotions is implicated. The Buddhist view of emotions is a part of a soteriology of liberation meant to alter our delusionary emotional responses.

More fully, for the Buddhist, emotions associated with selfishness and attachment are never "warranted."[12] What in ordinary English we refer to as "love," the Buddhist understands as either positive, neutral, or negative—depending upon its fine-grained nature as regards selfishness or overpowering attachment. If at love's root is overpowering, possessive attachment serving selfish interests, the Tibetan Buddhist considers it to be negative.

Buddhism holds that we do not pursue positive relationships for what we can gain for ourselves from the relationship. Selflessness is the underlying condition that runs through discussion of all cases of positive emotions. If a father and mother, for example, have real love for their child, they would help their child without the expectation that the child would do something for them when it grows up. Instead, they would help because they care for the child.[13] In a given relationship, even though it may appear that genuine care exists, we may find that at its root something quite selfish lies instead.

In the case of lovers, often positive affectionate care appears to exist. Two individuals might appear to be more devoted to each other than either one of them is to a parent, for example. But often, the care between parent and child is more genuine than a possessive lover relationship is. Often a person finds that possessive attachment underlies the relationship between lovers. That condition easily gives rise to jealousy. What may appear to be deep affection may quickly turn to aversion. The Buddhist agrees that as deep and caring a relationship can exist between lovers as between a normal parent and child. The Buddhist also agrees that a selfish relationship may turn into a positive selfless one where genuine positive caring love develops.

In contrast to possessive love, the Buddhist sees anger as a negative emotion. They liken anger to fire: immediate and destructive. They say that anger is the most destructive of the so-called delusions. We might counter that anger can have positive effects. But the Buddhist holds that, where it appears so, it is not the anger that has such effects. If other concurrent positive conditions did not exist, positive effects would not follow. Anger may well be mixed with a sense of fairness or justice, for example. That sense, not the anger, can lead to positive results.

My purpose in introducing these Buddhist views of emotion is to underscore the thought that our general view of emotions may significantly factor into how we frame a situation. How we frame a situation determines which emotions are or are not warranted.

7. Summary

I have not privileged the one-to-one or the one-to-many model. From incongruent emotions, depending on the case, we can reasonably posit one or more warranting reference frames. Along Davidsonian lines, we might counter that, instead of speaking of reference frames that warrant emotions, we should speak instead of different *reasons* for highlighting some features of a situation. Yet reference frames encapsulate Gestalt perceptions of a situation which reason-giving alone does not provide.

I have been speaking of the one-to-one model and of the one-to-many model between reference frames and warranted emotion(s). Two additional models deserve mention: many-to-one, and many-to-many. The many-to-one model is instantiated when different reference frames warrant a given emotion. For example, different reference frames may conspire simultaneously to warrant a given state of anger, as when a person simultaneously responds angrily to a marital situation and an unrelated military conflict. The many-to-many condition is instantiated when many reference frames simultaneously warrant many emotions. This last model effectively amounts to the one-to-one model.

We should not take the one-to-one model to be paradigmatic, although it might be useful to adopt it as an analytic starting point. Upon identifying an emotion, we may seek the operative reference frame that would warrant it. In the first instance, we may seek a single operative reference frame. Then we may discover that more than one reference frame warrants different anger states, say perhaps experientially melded together in an undifferentiated anger. In the extreme, when reference frames appear to conspire in this way, the anger might well take on a generalized dimension. Correspondingly, we might speak about such positive emotions as delight or joy when the collected reference frames give rise to a generalized sense of delight or joy, well being or bliss. The reconstruction of undifferentiated anger or undifferentiated delight may uncover the fact that the anger or delight is warranted from many cooperating reference frames. While the management of emotions may be served in the first instance by the one-to-one model, we have no reason to rule out the one-to-many model or the many-to-one model as analytically useful.

Let us review our findings: Different frames of an emotionally relevant kind may warrant different emotions or sets of congruent emotions and they may warrant complex incongruent emotions. Different reference frames may be incongruent, resulting in incongruent emotions. Mixed emotions typically mask different reference frames. A person may change emotions by changing reference frames. Reference frames are appropriate in accord with the narratives, programs, or projects, which motivate them. Finally, such narratives, programs, or projects accord with a favored view of emotions motivated by different interests and purposes.

Nine

ART AND SELF-TRANSFORMATION: CREATING AND BECOMING

While accounting for my epiphanic experience in my friend's studio, I introduced the idea of a personal program or project, or as I also call it, a personal mythology. What, more fully, is a personal program? To help situate ourselves to ourselves, Karl Popper suggests that we entertain programs for ourselves—life programs, if you will. Such a program or schematic map:

> with our own position marked on it, is part of our ordinary consciousness of self. It normally exists in the form of vague dispositions or programmes; but we can focus our attention upon it whenever we wish, whereupon it may become more elaborate and precise. This map or model is one of a great number of conjectural *theories* about the world which we hold and which we almost constantly call to our aid, as we go along and as we develop, specify, and realize, the programme and the timetable of the actions in which we are engaged.[1]

Accordingly, here is a sketch of my personal program. In answer to the question, why do I make art? I answer that I am engaged in self-transformation. My painting is instrumental to my self-transformation, and my self-transformation issues in my painting. My self-transformation and my production of art objects are integrally related. I value both painting and self-transformation as ends. Artistic production motivates my self-transformation and my self-transformation motivates my artistic production. At the same time, these two ends are symbiotically related, and while painting is a proximate aim, self-transformation is my ultimate aim.

I have already spoken about my epiphanic experience in the studio of a friend where, when being surrounded by her large abstract shaped canvasses, I experienced myself inhabiting the space depicted in them. I said that such inhabitation somehow forged an "inner" space with which I felt familiar. In the space of such non-duality, I suddenly became much more highly visually sensitive. As a consequence, I needed to paint—so that I might occupy the space of my own making. As a matter of inner necessity, I *had* to paint. After one year of intense production, I had my first one-person exhibition. This experience was not unlike that described by Wassily Kandinsky as an "inner necessity," or by Abraham Maslow as a "peak experience."[2] As a matter of my personal program, I have come to value this non-dualistic experience as a benchmark. I seek to perpetuate the self-transformation thereby experienced, and to seek vehicles—artistic, musical, philosophical—that foster it.

The idea of self-transformation—or, more explicitly, self-realization—carries with it the idea of progress. But according to what measures might there be progress? I suggest that, as in my visual epiphany, progress occurs if I come to experience more perspicuously, more expansively, more wakefully, perhaps more blissfully.[3]

Yet an artist may "freeze" his or her artistic development by mechanically replicating art objects because their prototype may be well received by the public. In this way, an artist may become mannerist. Persons may "freeze" their self-transformation much as they might freeze a moment in a human relationship in order to possess it. In such cases, persons' art and their individual selves become lifeless.

Consider again my epiphanic episode at the foot of Mount Vesuvius when a blissful sense of non-duality overcame me. I experienced a connectedness with the environment that was exhilarating and frightening. Then I cut the experience short, choosing not to be present for it. I summoned my rational faculties and raised questions. I began to doubt. The moment passed. I was afraid that the impending change would lead me into such unfamiliar territory that I might lose my bearings, my self-control. Later, though, I came to embrace the thought that my real work is my self-realization.

The idea of art making as self-transformative finds expression in the attitudes of such American Action Painters as Jackson Pollock, Lee Krasner, Franz Kline, and Willem DeKooning. They considered their resultant physical items as part of "act-paintings" whose metaphysical substance was regarded as identical with the artist's existence. Harold Rosenberg puts it this way:

> At a certain moment the canvas began to appear to one American painter after another as an arena in which to act—rather than a space in which to reproduce, re-design, analyze, or 'express" an object, actual or imagined . . . the big moment came when it was decided to paint . . . just to PAINT. . . . The painting itself is a "moment" in the adulterated mixture of (the artist's) life. . . . *The act-painting is of the same metaphysical substance as the artist's existence.* The new painting has broken down every distinction between art and life.[4]

The idea of circumscribing one's acts or one's existence as *works of art* is closely related to one which John Dewey describes when he says:

> We have *an* experience . . . when the material experienced runs its course to fulfillment. Then and only then is it integrated within and demarcated in the general stream of experience from other experiences. A piece of work is finished in a way that is satisfactory; a problem receives its solution; a game is played through; a situation, whether that of eating a meal, playing a game of chess, carrying on a conversation, writing a book, or taking part in a political campaign, is so rounded out that its

close is a consummation and not a cessation. Such an experience is a whole and carries with it its own individualizing quality and self-sufficiency. It is *an* experience.[5]

Accordingly, I have come to think of my artwork as the *process of the making*, culminating in art products and their effects in experience. Accordingly, I am partly "carried" by the development of my art products. When making an art product, I characteristically encounter unintended emergent features. Sometimes those emergent features are welcome; sometimes they are not. On occasion, I discover unintended linear or color relationships. On occasion, I discover scenes that point to fresh self-transformative opportunities.

On the other hand, Picasso tells an amusing story that illuminates emergent but *unwelcome* features in connection with a cubist painting being made by George Braque. He says:

> I remember one evening I arrived at Braque's studio. He was working on a large oval still life with a package of tobacco, a pipe, and all the usual paraphernalia of Cubism. I looked at it, drew back and said, "My poor friend, this is dreadful. I see a squirrel in your canvas." Braque said, "That's not possible: I said, "Yes I know, it's a paranoiac vision, but it so happens that I see a squirrel." . . . Braque stepped back a few feet and looked carefully and sure enough, he too saw a squirrel. . . . Day after day Braque fought that squirrel. He changed the structure, the light, the composition, but the squirrel always came back . . . However different the forms became, the squirrel somehow managed to return. Finally, after eight or ten days, Braque was able to turn the trick and the canvas again became a package of tobacco, a pipe, a deck of cards. . . .[6]

Just as a single work may give rise to emergent features, so too may a *series* of related works do so. These features may become apparent when the series is viewed as a whole, as in a solo exhibition. The recognition of such features may challenge both my ideas about my art objects and my self-transformation. Accordingly, I conceive of my artistic development in terms of my self-transformation. I regard the making of art objects as part of this larger process of becoming, one that is continuous and open-ended. That, more fully, *is the work.* Dewey says that such a transformative attitude obtains when there exists:

> complete interpenetration of self and the world of objects and events. Instead of signifying surrender to caprice and disorder, it affords our sole demonstration of a stability that is not stagnation but is rhythmic and developing.[7]

This "interpenetration of self and world of objects and events" is a condition of non-duality. Chang Chung-yuan articulates it when he asks, "What is Tao-painting?" He answers:

> *Tao* is the ontological experience by which subjective and objective reality are fused into one. . . . When the Chinese artist says that he enters the spiritual court he speaks of the ontological experience, the state of no-thought. This experience leads inevitably to the *interfusion of subjective and objective reality*. This interfusion initiates the process of creativity, which in turn establishes unity in multiplicity, the changeless in the ever-changing. The artist who has reached this state of oneness is supported by all the powers inherent in multiplicities and changes, and his work will be far beyond what his ego-form self could accomplish. Robert Henri (1865-1929), speaking of modern art, expresses somewhat the same idea: The object, which is back of every true work of art, is the attainment of a state of being, a state of high functioning, a more than ordinary moment of existence. In such moments activity is inevitable, and whether this activity is with brush, pen, chisel, or tongue, its result is but a by-product of this state, a trace, the footprint of the state. The work of art is, indeed, the by-product of a state of high functioning. This state of spiritual exaltation is fundamental to creative activity, while skills and measurements are secondary. It is the manifestation of an ontological experience.[8]

Ironically, trying to "own," or to freeze, or to possess such moments of the interfusion of subjective and objective reality (as Chang Chung-yuang puts it) can inhibit their very possibility. For the possessive impulse only affirms and entrenches the place of the "self" in opposition to the "other."[9] Duality reasserts itself.

Moments of non-duality or at-oneness between self and other, between artist and art-product, can be episodic in an unfolding career of artistic development and self-transformation. Such moments are relatively rare. But their existence calls into question any fixed distinction between artistic development and self-transformation.

I have come to think of my painting as instrumental to my self-transformation and my self-transformation as instrumental to my painting. According to my personal program (or my personal mythology) they are functionally the same. In response to this program, John Albin Broyer usefully remarks:

> There appears to be a deep religious undercurrent flowing through [Michael] Krausz's [account], and especially in his frequent use of the term "at-one." It would seem that the obvious correlation between his use of "at-one" and the religious use of the term *atone*ment to describe people's quest for over-coming fragmentation in their lives through reconciliation, is more than coincidental. George Santayana and John Dewey

are among the few contemporary philosophers with sufficient intellectual rigor and aesthetic sensitivity to develop viable hypotheses about the relationship of aesthetic consummation and religious meaning. Krausz could suggest the possibility that creative self-development through artistic-aesthetic expression may be one avenue for understanding the "religious" experience of atonement. If so, the import of art for self-development would make the "beauty" of art a functional *consequent* of its human meaning, rather than its *antecedent*, as is often supposed. "Beauty" would reside neither in the art object nor in the beholder alone, but would emerge as a definition of individual (and in "great" art, social) atonement.[10]

I have so far been speaking about my personal program, which addresses the question, why do I paint? Yet quite apart from this sort of personal program there remains the question as to how one should critically evaluate art products. James Munz, for example, notes:

> [Krausz] appears to assume that the standards appropriate for judging one's artistic production are also appropriate for judging one's self-development. But . . . if artistic production and self-development are separate ends, there is no reason that their standards are identical.[11]

Munz is right to suggest that standards of artistic development are distinct from those of self-realization. But they may be related in the way that Chang Chung-yuang describes when he speaks of the state of "high functioning" or "spiritual exaltation." If at-oneness involves an interpenetration of the subjective and the objective, the fixed distinction between artistic development and self-realization—along with their putatively independent measures—is called into question. A value that overrides the measures of both artistic production and self-realization may well exist, namely, as Broyer says, to overcome the fragmentation of life through reconciliation or atonement. Such a soteriological value is exemplified in Hindu, Buddhist, Taoist, and other traditions. Such a value collects the measures of artistic production and self-realization within a more encompassing field.

I have called upon this personal program or personal mythology to help motivate and to make sense of my artistic activity. More generally, a personal program is *mythic* in the sense that it presents a scenario or a possibly adoptable "picture." Its primary function is heuristic and motivational. The articulation of such a personal program helps me to locate my self in relation to my artistic efforts and the products they generate. Others may see their artistic activity in quite different ways. No single right way to think about such things exists.

Ten

SELF-TRANSFORMATION AND
LIMITS OF INTERPRETATION

I have argued that any object of interpretation—to be an object of interpretation—must answer to identity conditions. It must be countable. In order to be countable, it must be cast within the terms of some reference frame. As an example of "something beyond interpretation," I offer the case of the Vedantic notion of a Supreme Self. I offer it neither as a point of endorsement nor rejection, but as a case that exceeds the reach of interpretation. By extension, should other soteriologies or theologies invoke analogous notions, they too, would be beyond interpretation. Interpretation is concerned with elucidation and its attendant concerns for admissibility or validation in a general sense. Accordingly, rhetorical, or even physical, violence over the question of rightness or admissibility arises from a category mistake. But for purposes of this study, the case of the Vedantic Supreme Self is offered as an example that exceeds interpretability.

According to some soteriologies, the individual self is "realized" when it transcends all dualities. If the individual self is realized in this sense, it is transformed beyond all reference frames. Consequently, all talk of rightness or admissibility of interpretations of it would drop out. The limits of interpretive activity would have been overstepped. I will unpack this thought in the remainder of this chapter. In the first section, as a specimen view of the individual self, I will rehearse a narratist account. In the following sections, I will discuss its relation to a view of the non-individual "Supreme Self" embedded in a representative Vedantic soteriology.

1. Individual Self

Elsewhere I have argued for a narratist view of the individual self in contrast to a substantivist (or soul) view of the individual self.[1] I return to it here not so much to argue for it again as to provide a sample of a view about the individual self, to provide the terms for articulating some paradoxes that arise in a contrasting view of the Supreme Self. I stress at the outset that by outlining the paradoxes that arise from the Supreme Self view, I mean to demonstrate only its *uninterpretability* and thereby to indicate a limit of interpretive activity. That limit is the overriding concern of this chapter.

I argued that an individual self's antecedent potentialities are posited in light of present actualities. The present self retroactively posits its prior potentialities in light of the knowledge of the present actual. Accordingly, I affirmed that no innate unactualized substantive self exists that, through time, becomes actual. No past potential substantive self pre-exists before realization. No dormant essential unrealized self is *there* awaiting to be realized. The subject of the story is no inherent being but is a construction of the presently told story.[2] The individual self comes to be in the process of its own telling or expressing. By so doing, it creates the narrative space in which it inhabits. Accordingly, no self can exist without being a person. But a person can exist without a self, a person without self-narration.

Our individual self is constituted in the stories and episodes we deem significant, stories we tell about ourselves to ourselves and to others, in tandem and negotiation with stories that others tell about us. The shapes of our present stories depend upon how its elements relate and cohere. Accordingly, in such future perfect locutions as, "I will have experienced bliss" we cannot automatically assume that the identity of the projected self will be the same as the present narratizing self. No assumption of permanence or endurance can be sustained through time, for whether the present reference frame will have transformed in the duration is open. Andreea Deciu Ritivoi elaborates such a narratist view of individual self-identity when she says:

> [The narratizing self] structures lived experience into a coherent and meaningful configuration that makes individuals recognizable to themselves and to others. . . . From a narrative perspective, change, no matter how radical, can be contained in a single framework provided that disparate or contradictory events can be connected in a plot. Plots are . . . complex interpretive patterns that function in accordance with a logic of motivation and relevance. . . . Detecting such connections requires interpretive work that can establish plots that mediate between disparate components of action—chance occurrences, unfulfilled intentions, unknown causes, unexpected effects—and the temporal unity of the story recounted.[3]

Accordingly, the narratizing individual self creates the space in which its own identity is found and fostered. And the space created is a public space in the sense that it implicates the real or postulated listening "other." The individual self exists through its relations with others—others too as products of pertinent and relevant narratives. Ritivoi says:

> what a relevant community believes about a person (who they think she is, what they take her defining characteristics to be, how they evaluate her competence on a given matter, and how they locate her beliefs, values, and actions on their ethical scale) informs both the design and the reception of the person's communications and actions.[4]

Pertinent narratives, in accord with a logic of motivation and relevance, may accommodate disparate or opposing events that can be connected in a plot. The narratist is constrained not by an otherwise presumed fact of the matter independent of interpretive activity. Instead, the narratist is constrained by the relative coherence of the recounted story. Accordingly, this narratist view construes such phenomena as "self-deception" in terms of the unsustain-ability of incoherent narrative configurations that otherwise make individuals recognizable to themselves and to others. In this vein, Louis Mink tells us that self-narratives:

> must be compatible with and complement other narratives which overlap or are continuous with them. Even if there are different ways of emplot-ting the same chronicle of events, it remains true that . . . [such] narra-tives are capable of *displacing* each other. This happens, for example, when a narrative makes sense of a series of actions by showing them to be decisions reflecting a consistently held policy, where received ac-counts could only describe them as arbitrary and surprising reactions, or as irrational responses.[5]

So understood, the results of psychotherapeutic practices, for example, characteristically involve rehearsing, rejecting, modifying, or adopting narrative constructions in light of considerations of presently held beliefs and values. Notice that in such practices, two related yet distinct aims are characteristically pursued simultaneously, namely to "make sense" or elucidate the self and to "transform" or edify itself. Both these aims implicate some reference frames.

Yet—as I will elaborate presently—when the individual self pursues programs of self-transformation that seek to overcome its own *individuality*, whether, in the name of a Supreme Self, the individual self will have been abrogated, is an open question. If so, the distinction between the individual self and the Supreme Self will have been erased. The individual self no longer would seek to resolve individual crises, realign unsatisfactory behavioral patterns, or overcome disharmonies. Instead, for the seeker who pursues a path toward "self-realization" in a non-individuable Supreme Self, the pre-sumption of individuality in such efforts would drop out. Accordingly, per-sons who seek liberation by realizing that their true nature lies in non-individuality—for example by reciting the mantra, "Thou Art That," and by pursuing its associated meditative practices—purportedly find their true na-ture beyond the reach of all reference frames. From within the reference frame of individuality, the still unrealized individual self may offer reasons for exiting from that reference frame. Yet while individual selves may have offered reasons—as reasons—for pursuing such a soteriological path, they too drop out for one who (putatively) will have realized the promised state. Later in this chapter, I will discuss features of this sort of soteriological path. But first let us round out our discussion of the narratist view of individual selves.

According to the narratist view of the individual self, no pre-existent in-dividual autonomous self is *there,* awaiting interpretation. Instead, it is consti-

tuted in interpretive activity. Further, it is constituted and takes on its identity
by virtue of the reference frames in which it is nested. We have some choice
as to which reference frames to adopt and inhabit. We have some choice about
which "personal programs" or "personal mythologies" or personal "policies"
(as Mink might say) we adopt. To say that these programs or mythologies are
personal is not to say that no good reasons can be for accepting or rejecting one or another of these programs. Such choices need not be arbitrary or a
matter of whimsy.

More fully, personal programs are stories we tell ourselves about our
present place in relation to our presently reconstructed past and our projected
future, informed by our interests and purposes. In these stories, we place
ourselves to orient us to ourselves as we live our lives through its stages. As
David Novitz says:

> The construction of narrative identities, like that of works of art, is often
> highly inventive. Both are usually constructed with immaculate care, of-
> ten with insight and sensitivity, and in a way, moreover, which must al-
> ter and contribute to the sorts of people we are.[6]

Accordingly, when we speak of an individual *self in transition* we need
not assume that a substantive individual self in transition exists. I *find* myself
not, as the substantivist would have it, as a pre-narrative existent. Instead, I
find myself within the terms of an operative frame. Sometimes I may find
myself as constituted between two or more incongruent reference frames.[7] A
dramatic shift in a person's cultural surrounding, for example, may give rise
to different self-narratives. As a result—in pluralizing fashion—in the course
of such a transition a newly constituted self could be instantiated. One self
may become "lost" in the transition to the next self. Alternatively, a person
might find that a single individual self could have endured, but one that exhibits varying degrees of incongruent features.

The view that holds that the individual self is a narrative achievement,
the subject of its personal programs or mythologies, has a political dimension.
Novitz puts the point this way:

> There is an intricate political process at work here: what I should like to
> call the politics of narrative identity whereby we assert and maintain our
> own interests not just by advancing a particular view of ourselves, but
> by undermining the views that others advance of themselves. Stories and
> counterstories are told; history is written, subverted, and rewritten. And
> in this game of strategy, those who have the last word also have consid-
> erable power over those who do not.[9]

> [Such a story] . . . selectively mentions real or imaginary events, orders
> them in a developmental or sequential way (the plot), so that the whole

discourse (and the sequence of events which it mentions) eventually acquires a significance, usually a moral significance, from the way in which its parts are related to one another. . . . Without narrative, there is no way of emphasizing some events, marginalizing others, *and* at the same time relating all in a significant whole.[10]

Our narrative identities are neither God-given nor innate, but are painstakingly acquired as we grow, develop, and interact with the people around us.[11]

Insofar as we plausibly recount and adopt several incongruent narratives, the possibility that more than one individual self with "opposed" characteristics arises. As Mink suggests, the need and extent of their "resolution" depends upon our second-order requirements within our personal program as to whether a single self should answer to a single fully congruent narrative. As Novitz rightly says:

Most of us have, at best, a fragmented and changing view of self. We see ourselves successively in different, sometimes incompatible, ways, and we do so, on my view, because we are inclined to tell more than one story about ourselves.[12]

He continues, "The facts of my personal existence, the brute data of my life, do not themselves tell, or compel us to tell, any *one* story about myself."[13]

We may allow that the self in transition remains the same, perhaps by virtue of the consistency of a pertinent narrative. If I adopt a program for my self-realization—for realizing whom I ultimately am—I may presume that upon my arrival I will have been able to recall the aim that I had chosen to pursue. Yet at the earlier stage, I might not have had the conceptual resources even to imagine what it would be like to have arrived at such a realization. Or, upon realization we might have lost interest in the question of the original intent. The question may no longer be relevant. Or, we might have lost the resources it *would have taken* to recall the previous intending self. In the last case, a self would not even *tell* his or her story.

Notice that a person whose personal program involves self-realization that transcends individuality could concede the narratist view of the individual self as I have outlined it. But we would need to qualify such a concession. A person whose soteriology seeks realization of a Supreme Self that transcends the constraints of narrativity—including its dualities of subject and object—would find the question whether the narrative view of the individual self is adequate quite limiting. That person would regard the question as a diversion from the path to the Supreme Self.

2. Supreme Self

I will now address the idea of the Supreme Self more directly and more fully. The interpreter who aims to "make sense" or to elucidate a state of affairs assumes a role different from that of seekers who aim to edify or realize themselves. Those in the second category might seek to undo all dualisms—dualisms required for elucidation. Consequently, in meditative repose, such seekers must set aside interpretive activity. Theorizing about such activities as are associated with self-realization would (re-)install the very dualisms that would inhibit its transformational goals.

When interpreters utter the mantra, "Thou Art That,"—or its first person variant, "I am I"—they aim to elucidate a presumed state of affairs. In contrast, when seekers utter or meditate on the mantra, they aim to realize a state that promises to alleviate suffering. Paul Thom observes that seekers may pursue edificatory aims only if, when they regard the mantra as an assertion, they do not believe it to be false. As Paul Thom says:

> Consolation requires not knowledge but hope. A consoling message is not so much one we know that is true, as one we hope will be fulfilled. We must believe fulfillment of the message to be possible. But belief in a possibility is a far cry from knowledge. The consolations offered by the great religions often concern matters about which no knowledge is possible, one way or the other. Precisely because we cannot know that their claims are false, we can cling to the hope that they may be realized.[14]

The idea of self-realization is ambiguous, for the idea of realization is ambiguous. In one sense, we may realize or come to believe that a state of affairs obtains. In another sense, we may realize our potentialities. Such ambiguity marks two operative aims of self-realization. One aim is to elucidate what the self is. The other aim is to transform the self. The mantra, "Thou Art That," or, its first person variant, "I am I," is both elucidatory and transformative. These aims are noted by Krishna Roy when she says:

> The Indian philosopher does not stop short at the discovery of truth merely; he strives to realize it in his own outer and inner experience . . . [which] opens up the possibility of *moksa* or liberation.[15]

Of the mantra, "Thou Art That," Roy says:

> If we take the word "*tvam*" (thou) in the sense of an empirical individual limited to its body and the word "*tad*" (That) as the reality beyond the world, there can not be . . . identity between "*tvam*" and "*tad.*" . . . [I]t is only the pure consciousness of the individual soul that is identified with that in the universal soul.[16]

Swami Vivekananda says, "All is One, which manifests Itself, either as thought or life, or soul, or body, and the difference is only in degree."[17] In another place he says, "I am the birthless, the deathless, the blissful, the omniscient, the omnipotent, ever-glorious Soul,"[18] and in another, "All this manifoldness is the manifestation of that One. That One is manifesting Himself as many, as matter, spirit, mind, thought and everything else. It is that One, manifesting Himself as many."[19] He exhorts further, "Rise thou effulgent one, rise thou who art always pure, rise thou birthless and deathless, rise almighty, and manifest thy true nature."[20]

More fully, the recitation of the mantra involves not merely *asserting* that the individual conventional self is an embodiment of the Supreme Self. It also functions as an *enabling or transformative* vehicle, leading us to experience ourselves as an embodiment of *tad*. The dual aim of the recitation is to grasp the assertoric content of the mantra and to bring the interpreter to a higher level of consciousness. It is both *cognitive and transformative*. In the second sense, we understand it to liberate us from the afflictions suffered from the dualities of subject and object. Final realization brings refuge to the individual self who suffers from the false knowledge of its mortality. For in the final realization, no subject-object duality exists, no self-other duality, no duality at all. The conventional individual self is taken to be an embodiment or manifestation of that Supreme Self, the Absolute Self, the *Aatma*. The Absolute Self is the One, the infinite, the indivisible, the immutable, the eternal, the free, the pure, the Knowingness. The One, not a number in contrast with two or any other number, is beyond numerality or expression. So understood, any accounting of it—as attempted here, for example—must amount to a falsification.

Accordingly, self-realization is understood to be a process in which an individual self comes to *know* that he or she *is* the Supreme Self, a process in which the conventional individual self experiences itself as the Supreme Self. An individual's true Supreme Self does not cease, for his or her true nature is permanent. For the Supreme Self, no death occurs, for it was never born. Insofar as an individual self is a manifestation of the Supreme Self, the individual self was never born and does not die. It is immortal. In short, as Vibha Chaturvedi puts it:

> [Swami Vivekananda] takes the Advaita Vedantic doctrine of oneness of the ultimate reality as "The Truth." . . . In his view the ultimate aim of life is the realization of the *Brahman* where all consciousness of diversity and multiplicity is negated.[21]

3. Soteriological Paradoxes

I now turn to itemize paradoxes generated by such a soteriology. My concern in this account has been with a particular Vedantic orientation, that of Sankara (c. 788–820 or 850 CE), who affirms Oneness without duality, in contrast to

Ramanuja (c. 1017–1137 CE), who affirms a qualified monism.[22] (We find many alternative conceptions of the individual self and Supreme Self in Indian thought.) Keep in mind that I invoke it here primarily to thematize the overarching claim that an individual self is identified in terms of some reference frame. In the absence of such frames, it cannot count as an object of interpretation. The Supreme Self, the One, the *Aatma*, for which no identity conditions can be affixed, is uninterpretable. It cannot be an object of interpretation.

By paradox, I mean the sense associated with enigma, riddle, conundrum, contrariness to opinion, apparent absurdity on first hearing, or conflict with perceived notions of reasonableness. We may take up one of several attitudes in relation to a paradox. We may regard a paradox as either a mark of invalidity, to be rejected, as in a *reductio ad absurdum* argument; or, as a mark of insincerity on the part of its author, who cannot mean what he or she is saying; or, as a mark that its author is being ironic; or as a sign that the pertinent phenomenon is beyond received logics so we should resign ourselves to its nature. I suggest that the handling of a paradox may be informed by one's interests and purposes, be they the management of belief or self-transformation. In any event, I see no need to adopt a single general attitude toward paradoxes irrespective of interests and purposes.

Here, then, are eight paradoxes—or, I should say, clusters of paradoxes—that arise from the idea of self-realization as embodied in the mantra, "Thou Art That":

(1) Paradox of Self-Reference. The following paradoxes are articulated of necessity in some reference frame. So when we invoke the so-called Absolute—which is purportedly beyond all reference frames—we must invoke it from within a non-absolute or conventional reference frame. In so doing, we falsify the Absolute. Accordingly, when we elucidate a soteriology, which invokes the Absolute, we inhibit the pursuit of the edificatory path the soteriology sets for itself. Our elucidating the ends and means of such a soteriology at some stage undermines the achievement of the promised realization. At some stage, the program mandates a principled silence. As Ludwig Wittgenstein famously says in the last line of his *Tractatus*: "Whereof one cannot speak, thereof one must be silent."

Our elucidating a soteriology, which at some stage disqualifies elucidation, is incongruent with its aims. In this case, the twin aims of elucidation and edification are incongruent. They are pragmatically opposed. They entail different modes of engagement. This incongruence is reflected in the divergent attitudes we might take up with regard to the mantra, "Thou Art That," namely, the attitudes of assertion (elucidation) and transformation (edification). In the first case, we may take the mantra as a cognitive claim about the ultimate nature of things. In the second case, we may take it as a vehicle for self-transformation.

Chaturvedi tells us that Wittgenstein stresses the second attitude when he offers a non-cognitive or "picture" account of so-called religious belief:

[Wittgenstein] repeatedly warns against treating a religious belief as a scientific hypothesis. In his view, "believing" in religious contexts is a matter of having particular "pictures" that guide and regulate the thinking and life of the believer. The belief is a firm and unshakable belief not based on supporting evidence. Even where believers cite historical or other kinds of evidence, they treat this evidence quite differently and do not subject it to the kinds of checks to which they subject scientific and historical evidence. . . . if there were evidence it would destroy the whole business. Believing here is a matter of living your life according to particular pictures. . . . Wittgenstein observes: "It strikes me that a religious belief could only be something like a passionate commitment to a *system of reference*. Hence although it is belief, it is really a way of living or a way of assessing life.[23]

Wittgenstein points out that a nonbeliever does not contradict a believer. The believer does not accept something to be true that the nonbeliever contradicts. They are on different planes, they live differently and the pictures that regulate the believer's life have no role in the nonbeliever's life . . . theism and atheism are not to be seen as rival hypotheses or theories. We may extend this point to cover inter-religious and intra-religious differences in interpretation. We may say that different religious views should not be treated as rival theories about the same reality.[24]

Cast in our terms, the function of "assertoric" belief can inhibit the function of pertinent "pictures." Edification may be inhibited by elucidation. Chaturvedi characterizes the difference between cognitive and non-cognitive treatments of religious language when she says:

You may question whether different religious viewpoints, those pertaining to different religions and those pertaining to the same religion, should be seen as competing hypotheses or theories about a common, shared reality or world.[25]

If religious language is treated as non-cognitive, the difference and divergence can be explained as pertaining to differences in attitudes, feelings, moral commitments, and so on. But if religious language is said to involve assertions about the nature of reality, this diversity becomes greatly problematic, especially when we are confronted with diametrically opposed interpretations of the same object.[26]

(2) Paradox of Motivation. We may ask what might motivate the adoption of such a soteriology. The Vedantic soteriology holds that ultimate death does not apply to individual selves, for the individual self that would otherwise be thought to die is a manifestation of the timeless One. If death does apply to

the individual self, it does so "conventionally." But one's true nature is beyond the conventional self. (In contrast, Buddhists hold that all things are finally empty of inherent existence, including the individual self and the Supreme Self. Further, since they believe the Supreme Self to be empty of inherent existence, individual selves can be no embodiment of an inherent Supreme Self.)

One possible motivation for embracing a Vedantic soteriology may arise not so much from the fear of bodily death as from the fear of loss of individuality. Whatever else may survive after bodily death, I surmise—and it can only be a surmisal—that what *is* lost upon bodily death is individuality. This surmisal accords with R. G. Collingwood's remark, "If there is life after death, it must be so different from what we call "life" that it is misleading to call it by that name."[27]

With the gathering fear of loss of such individuality, this soteriology may be thought to offer a way to lose our individuality on our own terms. It provides a way to co-opt our conventional fate. By co-opting the loss of our individuality on our own terms, we affirm our freedom to do so. Alternatively, quite apart from the gathering fear of the fateful loss of individuality, this soteriology may be thought to alleviate the self of the "ordeal of individuality" within the terms of one's conventional existence. Such ordeals may include individual responsibility of many kinds.[28] Ironically, such motivations, as motivations, re-affirm the individual self.

Here is another possible motivation for adopting such a soteriology. Some sorts of lived experiences—what John Dewey calls "consummatory" experiences, what Abraham Maslow calls "peak experiences," what Mihaly Czikszentmihalyi calls "flow" experiences, or what Bernard Berenson calls "life enhancing experiences"—may be identified as meaning endowing. They include exceptionally arresting experiences of the self being at-one with an infinite Other, of an openness to an infinity. They include what is sometimes called aesthetic or religious experiences.[29] Arthur Danto describes these sorts of experiences as:

> high moments of artistic work [for example], those moments of pure creativity, when artist and work are not separated by a gap of any sort, but fuse in such a way that the work seems to bring itself into existence. At such points—and any creative person lives for these—there is none of the struggle and externality that marks those phases of artistic labor in which inspiration fails and the work itself refuses to cooperate. . . . [Brushes] are . . . agents of selflessness, which is the state at which . . . so much of Oriental philosophy . . . aims.[30]

We can view these sorts of experiences as revelatory of a deeper reality, a reality of which our conventional selves are manifestations. We may regard such experiences as touchstones for a consummatory or an enhanced way of life, one fashioned around the perpetuation of such experiences. Yet here again is the paradox of motivation. As motivations, these experiences entrench, not dissolve the individual self—which precisely goes counter to the aim of the soteriology.

(3) Paradox of Interpretability. Movement from the individual self to the posited Supreme Self involves a movement from a conventional reference frame to a frameless Absolute space. Interpretive activity can function at the conventional level only. Correspondingly, someone who is fully realized cannot interpret the One, for any attempt to do so would reinstall a dualism that would falsify the One.

In my discussion of narrativity, I suggested that the individual self can exist only in relation to pertinent reference frames. No fact of the matter about its identity exists independently of some reference frame. It follows that when we achieve full realization and when reference frames are lifted, no individual self can exist. Yet we may ask, when the "veils of dualisms" are lifted and then lowered again, can the individual self be lost *then* found again? Could it be the same individual self that then reappears? Can we move from the individual self to the Supreme Self, then again from the Supreme Self to the individual self? Can this process repeat itself indefinitely? Do the individual self and the Supreme Self appear simultaneously? I leave these questions for the reader to ponder.

We might say that movement from the individual self to the Supreme Self involves an abrogation of the individual self. We might say that upon realization we will have developed a sort of amnesia about where the individual self had first intended to go. Where the individual self had first intended to go would no longer matter. In that state of realization, the question whether the individual self had succeeded in getting to where it had wanted to go would have dropped out. It would have become irrelevant. As an individual self would have embarked on the path toward realization, he or she could not have *said* what the destination was because he or she could not fathom where such a self intended to go. Then, upon arrival, we could not say that the individual had successfully arrived because it would no longer be the sort of self that would intend in any relevant sense. So the question whether the original intention succeeded or failed is unanswerable.

So understood, the realization of the individual self involves its own abrogation. The individual self would have, but could not have been satisfied by its transformation to the Supreme Self. The would-be promise of enlightenment, made to the individual self, would have been undone when, upon its realization, the individual self would have been transformed. Promises to the individual self would have become inapplicable. Their fulfillments would no longer apply. The initial individual self would no longer be *there to* "accept" or *to* "experience" the promised fulfillment.

Analogously, whatever consolation the transformation might have promised, it could not console the individual self it was to have consoled. Ironically, the individual self, to which the promise of consolation would have been made, would no longer need consolation. The individual self would have been deconstructed. The notion of need would be inapplicable to the Supreme Self. In the movement from individual self to Supreme Self, the individual self would no longer be *there* to *be* consoled. So, with the realization of the Supreme Self, the initial motivating aim of bliss or enlightenment would drop out too. For the pursuit of bliss—as a pursuit—would inhibit its own possibility.

We might be tempted to suggest that the movement from the individual self to the Supreme Self involves a kind of *blasphemy*, where the individual self "presumptuously" assumes the place of the Supreme Self. Yet the idea of a realized being may, in turn, suggest the contrary: that for a person to deny that his or her true individual self *is* the Supreme Self, would be blasphemous. Such denial would demean both the Supreme Self and the individual self of which it is a manifestation, for "Thou *Art* That."

Further, we might ask whether, if the Supreme Self is so different from the individual self, to call the Supreme Self by a word so similar to the individual "self" is misleading. Alternatively, if we call the Supreme Self "Oneness" or "Being" then its appeal to the individual self as a promise for *its* liberation might become less apparent. Where, in the mantra "Thou art That," the "That" is understood as the One (as opposed to the Supreme *Self*), the identity claim between it and the individual self appears less natural. Using the same word, "self," in both cases suggests a continuous movement between the individual self and the Supreme Self. But the continuity of this movement appears not so easily sustained if we call Supreme Self, "Oneness" or "Being."

So far, when considering the mantra, "Thou Art That," we have considered a possible movement between an individual self and the Supreme Self. Yet if we hold that the individual self is a manifestation of the Supreme Self, we might allow the unorthodox view that several individual selves might be embodied in a single person and they may be manifestations of the Supreme Self. Perhaps not all the individual selves embodied in a single person are at the same time at the same stage in its realization that it is a manifestation of the One. This possibility raises interesting questions about the relation between those individual selves at different stages of realization and the dialogical spaces between them.[31]

(4) Paradox of Framing. We draw the distinction between the conventional and the Absolute from within a conventional field. We draw the distinction between frame-relativity and framelessness within a reference frame. For we can draw no distinction outside of some reference frame. But at the Absolute—where the distinction between subject and object drops out, and where the distinction between the conventional and the Absolute drops out—*any* characterization of self-transformation must also drop out. The Absolute, as articulated from within a conventional reference frame, must be a falsification of it. For the absolutist, no frames, no negations, no distinctions can exist. For the absolutist there can be no interpretation. Ironically, for the absolutist no absolutist can exist.

When the Vedantic philosopher speaks about sameness or difference, he or she must do so only from the conventional side. The idea of beyondness presumes a dualism. To say that something is beyond something else is to presume that we are talking about a difference in locations. So the effort to move beyond duality reinstalls itself at another level. Yet if we regard conventionality as a stage for its own transcendence, and we no longer remain concerned to articulate its relation to anything other than itself, then its paradoxicality loses its force.

Chaturvedi reports that, according to Swami Vivekananda, "the ultimate aim of life is the realization of the *Brahman* where all consciousness of diversity and multiplism is negated."[32] Where such realization obtains, no operative distinction between interpretation and its objects, or between such aims as elucidation or edification, can exist. So understood, the explicit pursuit of elucidation or edification could only be sustained at an intermediary conventional stage and not at the ultimate state of realization. In this way, for an individual self not fully realized, interpretive activity altogether could proceed only at a conventional level.

Yet, for the *interim* benefits it might bring, we might value the aim of final realization as desirable. At the conventional level, the aim of final realization might serve as a regulative principle. Such an aim might lessen the suffering of conventional existence, even if final realization is unachievable. Realization may remain partial and still offer some refuge.

(5) Paradox of Intentionality. Upon realization, what objects of consciousness can exist? Knowing, for example, is like such other intentional attitudes as being conscious, thinking, imagining, hoping, and desiring. A person cannot be conscious without being conscious *of* something. We cannot think without thinking *of* something. Individuals cannot imagine without imagining *something*. We cannot hope without hoping *for* something. We cannot desire without desiring *something*. All such attitudes take intentional objects. Knowing is no exception.

But the edificatory effect of the mantra, "Thou art That,"— in its fully realized state—involves deconstructing all intentional objects. With the deconstruction of all intentional objects we cannot successfully adopt any intentional attitude. For example, where no distinction between self and other or no distinction between knower and known exists, no knowledge can exist; for knowledge is inherently dualistic. The idea of "knowingness" is unintelligible without the distinction between knower and known. In the state of realization, knowingness in any recognizable sense cannot apply.

We can extend this point. Experience is also an intentional attitude. Individual selves cannot experience without experiencing *something*. Because of that duality, in the fully realized state—where the self merges with the Supreme Self (becomes One), obliterating the distinction between experiencer and experienced—"experience" can take no object; it ceases to exist. Yet, after the equipoise, an individual might tell a "falsifying" story about the so-called experience of realization the individual was supposed to have had. Such story telling would involve a re-installation of a subject-object duality.

Here is a related point. In the context of religious experience, whether two persons who purport to experience the same thing are actually doing so is contestable. Different interpretations of such purported experiences may be of different things. As Chaturvedi observes:

> The same experience of undifferentiated unity comes to be interpreted in different ways depending on the culture and religion to which the interpreter belongs . . . in the case of religious experiences you can challenge the contention that different people had the same kind of experiences.[33]

Religious experiences or "experiences of undifferentiated unity" (as Chaturvedi refers to them) do not come with unambiguous identity conditions. They resist judgments of sameness between two or more persons. Chaturvedi emphasizes the point when she says:

> [I]n cases of mystical or religious experiences, the possibility of diversity would arise only when it can be shown that the same kind of experiences lie behind different religious traditions. If the objects of interpretation were taken to be different, a crucial consequence of this admission would be that no religious tradition would be able to claim universal validity.[34]

Returning to the question of intentional objects, we may pause when considering perhaps the special case of bliss. One promise of the dissolution of the subject-object duality is that it brings bliss. We can be joyful *about* something. We can be happy or glad *about* something. We can be delighted *by* something. We can be ecstatic *about* something. But is bliss *about* anything at all? Is bliss an intentional attitude? Does it take an intentional object? If it does take an intentional object, however generalized or attenuated, it cannot fulfill the condition of "non-duality." Yet whether bliss is an intentional attitude, and whether it does involve an intentional object, however attenuated, remains an open question. For, what sense would it make to say "I bliss so-and-so," in a way parallel to "I imagine so-and so," "I think that so-and-so," or "I hope for such-and-such," and so on? Even at a stage where an individual is not fully realized, bliss may still take no intentional objects, not even attenuated ones.

Love may also be a special case. In its conventional sense, love is also an intentional attitude. We may love someone or some thing. But what of non-personal or non-individual love? Does a discernible intentional object exist in such loves, however attenuated? Consider the guru-teacher who loves his or her devotees for the manifestations of the One that he or she takes them to be. The individual devotee may be disappointed for not being loved for his or her individual self. He or she is loved for being an embodiment of the Supreme Self. Yet the disappointment may subside when, to retrieve the Guru's love, the individual perceives such love as an invitation to realize and become the Supreme Self. Accordingly, the guru's love may serve as a motivating vehicle for transformation. Paradoxically, the devotee may set aside his or her individuality to become the object of the guru's love. But then, when the devotee gives up individuality, can he or she be loved in any recognizable sense of love? Does any impersonal or non-individual love exist? Is it so different from what we usually call love that it might be best to call it something other than love?

Alternatively, can love, like bliss, be something that takes no intentional objects? Is bliss, after all, not an intentional attitude? Must we finally agree that intentional attitudes take a determinate non-attenuated intentional object? Perhaps a special kind of love, like bliss, takes no an intentional object. Perhaps, in the utterance, "I love you," "I" and "you" might be taken not as individuals but as place holders and vehicles toward a state without subject or object, expressed perhaps better in the passive voice, "love is going on." Or, if love requires any object, might its object be "all that exists." Perhaps that is behind the idea of love of God.

Consider further the idea of love of God as love of something completely attenuated, without bounds. But if love of God has no bounds, it cannot be an intentional object. So it cannot be the object of love in any recognizable sense. For this reason, we might be tempted to retreat to less attenuated objects. Though it might falsify to do so, we might postulate icons thought to reflect aspects of God. We might see a personalized or objectified form as an embodiment of a fully attenuated God, and—admittedly inadequate—may satisfy the need to love God which we cannot experience in its fully unattenuated state. In any event, apparently, we cannot succeed in loving God as fully attenuated, as fully objectless. If we wish to love God, we may need to objectify in order to have an unattenuated object to love.

Accordingly, we might postulate a continuum from determinate objecthood to non-objecthood. Between these poles are degrees of attenuated objects. The Vedantic tradition, for example, gives priority to the Supreme Self that is altogether non-objectual, and moves from that point to the more "mundane" intentional objects. The not-yet realized person starts with mundane objects and then moves toward the objectless. Yet what it is with which we would be confronted, when no intentional object remains, is vague. What, after all, is "pure awareness," "pure consciousness," pure freedom," "pure love," or "pure joy"? If such pure attitudes take no object whatever, they must be so different from what we usually call their mundane cousins (awareness *of*, consciousness *of*) that to call them by such similar names as consciousness (of), freedom (for, or from), love (of), or joy (about), is misleading.

(6) Paradox of Self-Recognition. One way to understand movement toward self-realization involves the thought that the conventional individual self *recognizes* that it is, or is a realization of, the Supreme Self. Recognition is an

intentional attitude. It takes an intentional object. When we recognize at all, we recognize something or other. So, if all dualisms have been overcome, no intentional attitudes could operate. No recognition would apply. Only the conventional self may recognize anything. Ironically, any recognition by a conventional self that might occur would impede the movement toward full realization.

The idea that a conventional self may recognize that it is, or is a manifestation of, the Supreme Self suggests that *re*-cognizing is occurring, some kind of *re*-collection. Because recognition is intentional, only the individual conventional self can re-cognize or re-collect. But if the idea of realization does involve bringing to consciousness what was already "innately known"— namely that one is, or is a manifestation of, the One—then what was originally known could have been known only by a conventional self. The recollection could not have been a recollection of a realized One at all. The conventional self cannot recognize that it is the Supreme Self. It cannot recognize its conventional self in the Supreme Self.

Otherwise, to know that I am, say, a kind of inquiring or seeking self requires being bounded by the intentionalities of inquiring and seeking. To recognize or recollect that I am such a kind of being implicates just the sort of intentionalities that should have been overcome in moments of putatively "true" self-recognition. Insofar as an individual self is defined and made intelligible to the self in the context of some reference frame, and insofar as the realized state involves the dissolution of all reference frames, the conventional self cannot recognize that it is, or is a manifestation of, the One. In this way, "I am I" (the first person version of "Thou Art That") appears to thwart itself.

But it might be objected that realization of Oneness need not involve recognition. Not all "parts of the individual self" need to be the product of intentional activity, or take intentional objects. This thought concedes that recognizing is an intentional attitude that could "thwart" the realization of Oneness. But such realization may be "beside" recognition. The relation between the individual self and the One may not be something to be re-cognized. What the individual self is, or comes to be, may include features it will be unable to re-cognize. At the same time, to concede that some features of the individual self may be unrecognizable does not rule out its *being* a feature of it. In this way, the individual self may *come to see* (although not re-cognize) the Oneness within itself, "something that is and is not of itself."[35]

(7) Paradox of Rationality. The distinction between the conventional and the absolute is intelligible only from within the reference frame of the unrealized. So if we can say anything at all (or point to) from within the conventional frame about what is beyond it, we can do so only in the negative. Speaking positively of the Absolute from the conventional reference frame falsifies it. We cannot speak positively of that which is beyond the conventional. We must "pass over" it in silence.

So understood, the One, the falsely understood "object of interpretation," cannot be interpreted. The closer we comes to it, the more attenuated it becomes, until, finally, we can say nothing at all about it. The conceptual resources for its would-be understanding would not apply. We could no longer even point.

But rational thought altogether involves subject-object dualities. It involves assertions of truth or falsity, admissibility or inadmissibility, and the like. It involves distinguishing between what a thing is from what it is not. So if we overcome all dualities, rational thought drops out too. The most general reference frame we might adduce is that of rationality. Notice that the justification of rationality is circular in the sense that any reasons given in its support already assumes rationality. Yet, despite such question beggingness, we might give reasons to justify rationality. The reasons would be inconclusive in the sense that they are internally ampliative. They flesh out what behaving in a rational way is like without presuming that such demonstration is grounded in a neutral space.[36] Still, we can exercise the choice to exit from rational thought only from the conventional rational side. One sort of reason why we might be tempted to exit from rational thought is inductive. Upon the gradual or periodic deconstruction of subject-object dualities, we might have bliss-like (or "flow-like") experiences. Accordingly, we might project (rightly or wrongly) that with full and permanent deconstruction of all dualities, we would have full and permanent bliss.

We have already touched upon the allusiveness of such a projection. But the choice to exit rational thought altogether is resisted by Nelson Goodman, for example, who expresses his opposition to all forms of mysticism in this way:

> I hear the anti-intellectualistic, the mystic—my arch enemy—saying something like this: "Yes, that's just what I've been telling you all along. All our descriptions are a sorry travesty. Science, language, perception, philosophy—none of these can ever be utterly faithful to the world as it is. All make abstractions or conventionalizations of one kind or another, all filter the world through the mind, through concepts, through the senses, through language; and all these filtering media in some way distort the world. It is not just that each gives only a partial truth, but that each introduces distortions of its own. We never achieve even in part as really faithful portrayal of the way the world is."[37]

As Goodman sees it, mysticism is the claim that a world beyond the reach of any reference frames of knowing exists. Goodman rejects this notion. My aim here is not to defend Goodman's intellectualism over mysticism as he understands it. I suggest only that those who embrace mysticism jettison all reference frames which are, in turn, necessary for *interpretive activity* to operate at all.

Yet when we regard the mantra in its elucidatory or assertive mode, we might ask whether it is *true* that "Thou Art That." Is it true that individual selves are embodiments of the One, the Supreme Self? Can we say? After all, under what intersubjectively sharable conditions could we corroborate or refute such a proposition? What would count as confirmation or disconfirmation? Even if we succeeded in overcoming subject-object dualities, does that amount to having realized the One? Is the overcoming of all dualities sufficient for the realization of Oneness? Could we have overcome all dualities and still not have realized Oneness? Ironically, the question whether the subject-object duality has been overcome presumes the subject-object duality in question. The question reinstates the duality that would have been deconstructed. Inter-subjective accountability presupposes the very subject-object duality which is what full realization is supposed to deconstruct.

At the stage of full realization, the distinction between conventional truth and absolute truth cannot operate. Truth could operate only at interim stages. Since truth is dualistic, it can operate at the conventional level only, not at the Absolute level. Truth can be no part of the vocabulary of the Absolute.

(8) Paradox of Truth and Oneness: Within the terms of the soteriology we have been considering, Oneness is generally understood as beyondness of all dualities, including the duality of truth and falsity. Taken this way, the embrace of Oneness "as true" entails that we are denied the possibility of asserting it as true. Alternatively, we may embrace Oneness for its transformational value, for its power to dissolve the ego-self as it moves toward the realization of "pure freedom," "pure love," or "pure awareness." Yet here, too, dualism re-emerges. For this alternative suggestion is a bit of practical reasoning: "Do A as a means to achieve B" presupposes the duality of A and B. In the process of realization, at some stage, practical reasoning is also deconstructed. If pure freedom is the aim, it is an aim designated from the side of the conventional self. It can be no aim of the Supreme Self in whose space no aims exist. Within the terms of the soteriology here considered, the aim remains ineliminably conventional.

Even if we could not know the mantra to be true or false—for any inter-subjective account would beg the question in a dualistic direction opposed to the ultimate aim of the soteriology—that would not discount the *use* of the mantra as a vehicle for transformation to another—even if not fully realizable—level of consciousness.

We are left with the unanswerable questions whether the dissolution of all duality gives rise to pure realization. Does it instead give rise to emptiness? How could we tell? These questions are unanswerable for they are questions any one of whose answers we might affirm or deny. To do either would reinstall the duality we had set about to deconstruct.

To recapitulate, I have illustrated that the Vedantic (Sankara) tradition takes Oneness to be beyond predication, without individuating conditions. That to which the assertion of Oneness addresses is beyond the subject-object constraints of language. Oneness is beyond number. It is beyond the limits of interpretation, for it can be no object of interpretation. We cannot judge Oneness to be the same or different from that which is affirmed in another tradition—Buddhist, for example—when the other tradition affirms the emptiness of inherent existence. Accordingly, Ken-ichi Sasaki observes:

> I doubt whether "Atma" or "Anatma" is given as an answer to the question concerning "the nature of things." Are they not instead [offering] the answer to a question too general, too fundamental, too comprehensive, and too universal for its subject to be determined . . . ? Are they not pure intuition without any object . . . or subject?[38]

If we cannot know whether the central tenets of different soteriological traditions are about the same or different things, and if we cannot know whether putative experiences are of the same or different things, then there can be no competition between claims about them. For any such competitions presuppose that different traditions address the same thing. Without such knowledge of sameness, the question of rightness or admissibility cannot arise. Without such knowledge any conflict—whether verbal or physical—is utterly misplaced.

The Vedantic (Sankara) notion of the Supreme Self is uninterpretable. That entails neither that we should or should not endorse it for whatever edificatory functions it may serve. But it does illustrate its disqualification as an object of interpretation.

More generally, if a putative object of interpretation lacks such identity conditions as would allow us to count it as one or more, it could answer to neither a singularist nor multiplist condition. It could be no object of interpretation. Insofar as interpretive activity is elucidatory in that it involves questions of admissibility and validation, it would be uninterpretable. Such is one limit of interpretation.

NOTES

Preface

1. Michael Krausz, *Rightness and Reasons: Interpretation in Cultural Practices* (Ithaca, N.Y.: Cornell University Press, 1993); and *Limits of Rightness* (Lanham, Md.: Rowman and Littlefield Publishers, 2000).
2. Andreea Deciu Ritivoi, ed., *Interpretation and its Objects: Studies in the Philosophy of Michael Krausz* Amsterdam: Rodopi Publishers, 2003); and Michael McKenna, *Interpretation and Culture: Themes in the Philosophy of Michael Krausz*, special issue, *Philosophy in the Contemporary World*, 12:1 (Spring–Summer 2005).

Introduction

1. Morris Weitz, "The Role of Theory in Aesthetics," *Journal of Aesthetics and Art Criticism,* 15 (1956), pp. 27–35.
2. Nirmalangshu Mukherji, "Is there a General Notion of Interpretation?" *Interpretation and its Objects: Studies in the Philosophy of Michael Krausz*, ed. Andreea Deciu Ritivoi (Amsterdam: Rodopi Publishers, 2003), p. 39.
3. Paul Thom, " Constituents of Interpretation," In Ritivoi. *Interpretation and its Objects*, p.116.
4. Ibid., pp. 116–117.

Part One: Interpretation

Chapter One

1. Michael Krausz, *Rightness and Reasons: Interpretation in Cultural Practices* (Ithaca, N.Y.: Cornell University Press, 1993); and *Limits of Rightness* (Lanham, Md.: Rowman and Littlefield Publishers, 2000).
2. Krausz, *Rightness and Reasons*, chap. 3; H. P. Brenner, "Introductory Appreciations," *Van Gogh in Perspective*, ed. Bogomila Welsh-Ovcharov (Englewood Cliffs, N.J.: Prentice Hall, 1974), p. 85; Griselda Pollock, "Van Gogh and the Poor Slaves: Images of Rural Labor as Modern Art," *Art History*, 11 (September 1988), pp. 406–409; H. R. Graetz, *The Symbolic Language of Vincent Van Gogh* (New York: McGraw Hill, 1963); and Albert Lubin, *Stranger on the Earth: A Psychological Biography of Vincent Van Gogh* (New York: Holt, Rinehart, and Winston, 1972).
3. Krausz, *Limits of Rightness,* pp. 19–24; Lisa Saltzman, *Anselm Kiefer and Art after Auschwitz* (Cambridge, UK: Cambridge University Press, 1999), pp. 122–123; and Rafael Lopez-Pedraza, *Anselm Kiefer: After the Catastrophe* (London, Thames and Hudson, 1996), pp. 13–16, 7.
4. Ernst Van De Wetering, "The Various Functions of Rembrandt's Self-portraits," *Rembrandt's Hidden Self-Portraits* (Amsterdam: Museum Het Rembrand-

thuis, 2003), pp. 27–41; quote from 28; and H. P. Chapman, *Rembrandt by Himself*, Exhibition Catalogue, (Glasgow Museums & Art Galleries, 1991), p. 13.

5. H. P. Chapman quoted in Van De Wetering, "The Various Functions of Rembrandt's Self-portraits," p. 29.

6. Ibid., p. 27, emphasis added.

7. Susan Fegley Osmond, "Rembrandt's Self-Portraits," *The World & I* (September Issue, January 2000), pp. 2–14, emphasis added.

8. Charles Taylor, *Sources of the Self: The Making of Modern Identity* (Cambridge, Mass.: Harvard University Press, 1980) quoted by Van De Wetering, in "The Various Functions of Rembrandt's Self-portraits,," p. 28.

9. Van De Wetering, "The Various Functions of Rembrandt's Self-Portraits," p. 30; and Taylor, *Sources of the Self*, p. 184.

10. Ibid., p. 40.

11. David Novitz, "Against Critical Pluralism," *Is There a Single Right Interpretation?* ed. Michael Krausz (University Park: Pennsylvania State University Press, 2002), p. 115; Alexander Nehamas, "The Postulated Author: Critical Monism as a Regulative Ideal," *Critical Inquiry*, 8 (Autumn 1981), pp. 133–149; and Monroe Beardsley, "The Authority of the Text," and E. D. Hirsch, "In Defense of the Author," *Intention and Interpretation*, ed. Gary Iseminger (Philadelphia, Penn.: Temple University Press, 1992).

12. Joseph Margolis, "Relativism and Interpretive Objectivity," *Metaphilosophy*, 31:1/2 (January 2000), p. 222.

13. David Crocker, "Interpretive Ideals and Truth Commissions," *Interpretation and its Objects: Studies in the Philosophy of Michael Krausz*, ed. Andreea Deciu Ritivoi (Amsterdam: Rodopi Publishers, 2003), p. 58.

14. Joseph Margolis, "Robust Relativism," *Intention and Interpretation*, p. 49.

15. Joseph Margolis, "The Truth About Relativism," *Relativism: Interpretation and Confrontation*, ed. Michael Krausz (Notre Dame, Ind.: Notre Dame University Press, 1989 and 1990), p. 251.

16. *The Compact Oxford English Dictionary*, 2nd ed. (Oxford: Oxford University Press, 1996), emphasis added.

17. Eric W. Weisstein, "Congruence," from MathWorld—A Wolfram Web Resource: http://mathworld.wolfram.com/Congruence.html (accessed 15 August 2006).

18. Ibid.

19. Nicholas Maxwell, "Art as its Own Interpretation," In Ritivoi, *Interpretation and its Objects*, pp. 278–279.

20. Edward J. Sozanski, "N.Y.C. Shuts the Gates on this Banal Public Art. Christo's Orange Drapes Were a Massive Superficial Success," Art, *The Philadelphia Inquirer*, 6 March 2005.

21. Miriam Hill, "The Gates," *The Philadelphia Inquirer*, 4 March 2005.

22. Peter Schjeldahl, "Gated,"*The New Yorker*, 28 February 2005, pp. 30–31.

23. Mark Stevens, "Curtain Up," *New York* (magazine) (28 February 2005), pp. 64–65.

24. Peter Lamarque, "Appreciation and Literary Interpretation," *Is there a Single Right Interpretation?* p. 306.

25. Maxwell, "Art as its Own Interpretation," pp 269–270, 272; and Leo Steinberg, *Leonardo's Incessant Last Supper* (New York: Zone Books, 2002).

26. Michael Podro, "Space, Time and Leonard," *Times Literary Supplement*, 4 January 2002.

27. Ibid., emphasis added.

28. Andrew Butterfield, "Leo's Last Supper," *The New York Review of Books* (18 July 2002), pp. 24–25, (emphases added).

29. Maxwell, "Art as its Own Interpretation," p. 276.

Chapter Two

1. Bernard Harrison and Patricia Hanna, "Interpretation and Ontology: Two Queries for Krausz," *Interpretation and its Objects: Studies in the Philosophy of Michael Krausz*, ed. Andreea Deciu Ritivoi (Amsterdam: Rodopi Publishers, 2003), p. 98.

2. Patricia Hanna, correspondence with author, 5, 10, and 12 April 2002.

3. Patricia Hanna, "Interpretation and Ontology: Do We Discover or Invent Reality?" (Unpublished paper), p. 10.

4. Harrison and Hanna, "Interpretation and Ontology," p. 99, 103–104.

5. Ibid., p. 106.

6. Ibid., p. 94.

7. Ibid., p. 104.

8. Rom Harré, "Is there a Basic Ontology for the Physical Sciences?" *Dialectica*, 51:1 (1997), pp. 17–33, esp. 32.

9. Nancy Weston, "Rightness, Ontology, and the Adjudication of Truth: Adumbrations from the Law's Trial," In Ritivoi, *Interpretation and its Objects*, p. 240, emphasis added.

10. Ibid., p. 242.

11. Ibid., p. 244.

12. Ibid., pp. 247–248.

13. Ibid., p. 248.

14. Andreea Deciu Ritivoi, "Interpreting Historical Legacies: The Ethos of Transition in Eastern Europe," In Ritivoi, *Interpretation and its Objects*, p. 212.

15. Weston, "Rightness, Ontology, and the Adjudication of Truth," p. 263.

Chapter Three

1. David Crocker, "Interpretive Ideals and Truth Commissions," *Interpretation and its Objects: Studies in the Philosophy of Michael Krausz, ed.* Andreea Deciu Ritivoi (Amsterdam: Rodopi Publishers, 2003), p. 58.

2. Ibid.

3. Vibha Chaturvedi, "Reflections on the Interpretation of Religious Texts," In Ritivoi, *Interpretation and its Objects*, pp. 308–309, emphasis added.

4. Bernard Harrison and Patricia Hanna, "Interpretation and Ontology: Two Queries for Krausz," In Ritivoi, *Interpretation and its Objects: Studies in the Philosophy of Michael Krausz, ed.* Andreea Deciu Ritivoi (Amsterdam: Rodopi Publishers, 2003), p. 97.

5. Chaturvedi, "Reflections on the Interpretation of Religious Texts," p. 307, (diacritical marks omitted).

Chapter Four

1. Paul Thom, "Constituents of Interpretation," *Interpretation and its Objects: Studies in the Philosophy of Michael Krausz*, ed. Andreea Deciu Ritivoi (Amsterdam: Rodopi Publishers, 2003), pp. 113–114.
2. Ronald Moore, "Interpretive Ideals and Life Projects," In Ritivoi, *Interpretation and its Objects*, p. 85, emphasis added.
3. Ibid., p.83.
4. David Novitz, "Against Critical Pluralism," *Is There a Single Right Interpretation?* ed. Michael Krausz (University Park: Pennsylvania State University Press, 2002), pp. 118–119.
5. Jitendra Mohanty, "Phenomenological Rationality and the Overcoming of Relativism," *Relativism: Interpretation and Confrontation*, ed. Michael Krausz (Notre Dame, Ind.: Notre Dame University Press, 1989 and 1990), pp. 333–334.
6. Peter Lamarque, "Object, Work and Interpretation," *Interpretation and Culture: Themes in the Philosophy of Michael Krausz*, special issue, ed. Michael McKenna, *Philosophy in the Contemporary World*, 12:1 (Spring–Summer 2005), pp. 5–6, (emphases added).
7. Peter Lamarque, "Objects of Interpretation," *Metaphilosophy*, 31:1/2 (January 2000), pp. 96–124, esp. 110.
8. Nicholas Maxwell, "Art as its Own Interpretation," In Ritivoi, *Interpretation and its Objects*, p. 269.
9. Ibid., p. 272.
10. Christoph Cox, "Versions, Dubs, and Remixes: Realism and Rightness in Aesthetic Interpretation," In Ritivoi, *Interpretation and its Objects*, pp. 286–287, emphasis added.
11. Ibid., pp. 288–290.
12. Ibid., p. 288.
13. Ibid., pp. 288–28.

Chapter Five

1. Nelson Goodman, "Just the Facts, Ma'am.," *Relativism: Interpretation and Confrontation*, ed. Michael Krausz (Notre Dame, Ind.: Notre Dame University Press, 1989 and 1990), pp. 84–85.
2. Joseph Margolis, "Robust Relativism," *Art and Philosophy: Conceptual Issues in Aesthetics* (Atlantic Highlands, N.J.: Humanities Press, 1980), p. 160, emphasis added.
3. Peter Lamarque, "Object, Work, and Interpretation," *Interpretation and Culture: Themes in the Philosophy of Michael Krausz*, special issue, ed. Michael McKenna, *Philosophy in the Contemporary World*, 12:1 (Spring–Summer 2005), p. 6, emphasis added.
4. Joseph Margolis, *Art and Philosophy* (Brighton, UK: Harvester University Press, 1980), p. 38, first emphasis added.

5. Chhanda Gupta, "Constructive Realism and the Question of Imputation," *Is There a Single Right Interpretation?* ed. Michael Krausz (University Park: Pennsylvania State University Press, 2002), p.157–158, emphases added.

6. Chhanda Gupta, "Explanation, Causation and Physical Necessity from the Standpoint of Internal Realism," (Unpublished paper), pp. 13–14.

7. Lucas Samaras, *Head Transformation* (set of 12, 1982), reproduced in Michael Krausz, *Rightness and Reasons: Interpretation in Cultural Practices* (Ithaca, N.Y.: Cornell University Press, 1993), pp. 124–125, courtesy of Pace Gallery, New York.

8. Chuck Close, *John*, (1998), in an exhibition entitled "Chuck Close Prints: Process and Collaboration," at the Metropolitan Museum of Art, New York City, 13 January–18 April 2004; and Terrie Sultan, ed., *Chuck Close Prints: Process and Collaboration*, (Princeton, N.J.: Princeton University Press, 2003), pp. 101–103.

9. Chuck Close, quoted in Richard Shiff, "Through a Slow Medium," *Chuck Close Prints*, p. 41.

10. Krausz, *Rightness and Reasons*, p. 123.

11. Karl Popper, "The Myth of the Framework," *The Abdication of Philosophy: Philosophy and the Public Good*, 1st ed. (Chicago, Ill.: Open Court Publishing Company, 1976), p. 40.

12. Ibid., p. 40.

Chapter Six

1. Donald Davidson, "On the Very Idea of a Conceptual Scheme," *Relativism: Cognitive and Moral*, eds. Jack Meiland and Michael Krausz (Notre Dame, Ind.: Notre Dame University Press, 1982), pp. 66–80.

2. Joseph Margolis, "The Truth About Relativism," *Relativism: Interpretation and Confrontation*, ed. Michael Krausz (Notre Dame, Ind.: Notre Dame University Press, 1989), p. 232; and "Interpretation, Relativism, and Culture: Four Questions for Margolis," *Interpretation, Relativism and the Metaphysics of Culture: Themes in the Philosophy of Joseph Margolis*, eds. Michael Krausz and Richard Shusterman (Amherst, N.Y.: Humanity Press, 1999), pp. 105–124.

3. Karl Popper, "The Myth of the Framework," *The Abdication of Philosophy: Philosophy and the Public Good*, 1st ed. (Chicago, Ill.: Open Court Publishing Company, 1976), p. 35.

4. Michael Krausz, *Rightness and Reasons: Interpretation in Cultural Practices* (Ithaca, N.Y.: Cornell University Press, 1993), chap. 3; and this volume, chap. 3.

5. Alasdair MacIntyre, "Relativism, Power, and Philosophy," *Relativism: Interpretation and Confrontation*, p. 199.

6. Karl Popper, "The Myth of the Framework," p. 46.

7. Ibid., p. 38.

8. Davidson, "On the Very Idea of a Conceptual Scheme," p. 67.

9. Ruth Benedict, *The Chrysanthemum and the Sword: Patterns of Japanese Culture* (New York and Scarborough: New American Library, 1974), p. 223.

10. Benjamin Lee Whorf, *Language, Thought, and Realty* (New York: Technology Press of MIT and John Wiley & Sons, Inc., 1962), pp. 243–244.

11. Davidson, "On the Very Idea of a Conceptual Scheme," p. 66.

12. Ibid., p. 74.

13. Ibid.

14. John McDowell, "Scheme-Content Dualism and Empiricism," *The Philosophy of Donald Davidson*, Library of Living Philosophers, vol. 27, ed. Lewis Edwin Hahn, (Chicago and LaSalle Illinois: Open Court, 1999), p. 96.

15. Davidson, "On the Very Idea of a Conceptual Scheme," p. 79.

16. Ibid., p. 66.

17. Ibid., p. 79.

18. Ibid., p. 72.

19. Ibid., p. 79.

20. Ibid., p. 68

21. David Wong, correspondence with author, 30 July 2003; Arthur Waley, *The Analects of Confucius* (New York: Vintage Books, 1989); D. C. Lau, *Confucius: The Analects* (London: Penguin, 1979); Wing-tsit Chan, *A Sourcebook in Chinese Philosophy* (Princeton, N.J.: Princeton University Press, 1969); and Roger Ames and Henry Rosemont, Jr., *The Analects of Confucius: A Philosophical Translation* (New York: Ballantine Books, 1999).

22. Alasdair MacIntyre, "Relativism, Power and Philosophy," pp. 188–189.

23. Ibid., pp. 189, emphasis added.

24. Hilary Putnam, "Truth and Convention: On Davidson's Refutation of Conceptual Relativism," *Relativism: Interpretation and Confrontation*, pp. 180–181.

Chapter Seven

1. Paul Thom, "Constituents of Interpretation," *Interpretation and its Objects: Studies in the Philosophy of Michael Krausz*, ed. Andreea Deciu Ritivoi (Amsterdam: Rodopi Publishers, 2003), p. 109.

2. David Novitz, "Art, Narrative, and Human Nature," *Philosophy and Literature*, 13:1 (April 1989), pp. 70–71.

3. Michael McKenna, "A Metaphysics for Krausz," In Ritivoi, *Interpretation and its Objects*, p. 133.

4. Ibid., p. 129.

5. Ibid., p. 130.

6. Ibid., p. 131.

7. Ibid., pp. 136, 138.

8. Ibid., p. 144.

9. Ibid., p. 134.

10. Ibid., p. 130.

11. Ibid., p. 141.

12. David L. Norton, *Imagination, Understanding, and the Virtue of Liberality* (Lanham, Md., 1996), pp. 84–85.

13. Bernard Harrison and Patricia Hanna, "Interpretation and Ontology: Two Queries for Krausz," In Ritivoi, *Interpretation and its Objects*, p. 98.

14. Ibid., p. 102; and Patricia Hanna and Bernard Harrison, *Word and World: Practice and the Foundations of Language* (New York and Cambridge: Cambridge University Press, 2004), pp. 353, 356.

15. Harrison and Hanna, "Interpretation and Ontology," p. 94.
16. Ibid., pp. 99–100.
17. Ibid., pp. 101–102.
18. Ibid., p. 103.
19. Ibid.
20. Bernard Harrison, "Language, Literature and Reality," paper presented at the American Philosophical Association, Pacific Division, Portland Oregon, March, 2006, p. 11; and Anat Mater, *Review of Patricia Hanna and Bernard Harrison, Word and World: Practices and the Foundation of Language* (Cambridge: Cambridge University Press, 2004), *Notre Dame Philosophical Reviews*, 10 November 2004, http://ndpr.nd. edu/review.cfm?id=1414 (accessed 13 August 2006).
21. Harrison, "Language, Literature and Reality," p. 8–9.
22. Ronald Moore, "Interpretive Ideals and Life Projects," In Ritivoi, *Interpretation and its Objects*, p. 81.
23. Bernard Harrison, Email communication with author, 8 May 2006.

Part Two: Transformation

Chapter Eight

1. Ronald De Sousa, "The Rationality of Emotions," *Explaining Emotions*, ed. Amélie Oksenberg Rorty (Berkeley: University of California Press, 1980), p. 133.
2. Ibid., p. 140, emphasis added.
3. Ibid., p. 145
4. Louis O. Mink, "Narrative Form as a Cognitive Instrument," *The Writing of History: Literary Form and Historical Understanding*, eds. Robert H. Canary and Henry Kozicki (Madison: University of Wisconsin Press, 1978), p. 147.
5. Ibid., p. 152.
6. Roy Schafer, "Action and Narration in Psychoanalysis," *New Literary History*, 12: 61–85 (1980), pp. 61–85, quote 47.
7. De Sousa, "The Rationality of Emotions," p. 146.
8. Rom Harré and Michael Krausz, "Moral Relativism," *Varieties of Relativism* (Oxford: Basil Blackwell, 1996), esp. chap. 5.
9. Bronwyn Davies and Rom Harré, "Positioning: The Discursive Production of Selves," *Journal of Theory and Social Behaviour*, 20:1 (1990), pp. 43–63, quote 46.
10. Michael Krausz, "Creating and Becoming," *The Concept of Creativity in Science and Art*, eds. D. Dutton and M. Krausz (The Hague: Martinus Nijhoff Publishers, 1981), p. 192.
11. Ibid., p. 191.
12. Lobsang Gyatso, founding Director of the Institute of Buddhist Dialectics in Dharamsala, India, interview with author, 28, 30, 31 May 1996.
13. Harry Frankfurt, *The Reasons of Love* (Princeton, N.J.: Princeton University Press, 2004).

Chapter Nine

1. Karl Popper and John C. Eccles, *The Self and Its Brain: An Argument for Inter-actionism* (London: Routledge & Kegan Paul, 1983), p. 91.
2. Wassily Kandinsky, *Concerning the Spiritual in Art, and Painting in Particular* (New York: Wittenborn, Schultz, 1963 [1921]); and A. H. Maslow, *Religions, Values, and Peak Experiences* (New York: Viking Press, 1963).
3. J. N. Findlay, "The Perspicuous and the Poignant," *Aesthetics*, ed. Harold Osborne (London: Oxford University Press, 1972).
4. Harold Rosenberg, "The American Action Painters," *Art News*, 51 (1952), pp. 22–23, 48, emphasis added.
5. John Dewey, *Art as Experience* (New York: Capricorn Books, 1934), p. 35.
6. F. Gilot and C. Lake, *Life with Picasso* (New York: McGraw-Hill, 1964), pp. 68–69.
7. Dewey, *Art as Experience*, p. 19.
8. Chang Chung-yuan, *Creativity and Taoism: A Study of Chinese Philosophy, Art and Poetry* (New York: Harper Colophon Books, 1970), pp. 203–4, emphasis added.
9. Erich Fromm, *To Have or To Be?* (New York: Harper and Row, 1976).
10. John Albin Broyer, Letter to the Editor, *Leonardo*, 13 (1980).
11. James Munz, Letter to the Editor, *Leonardo* 13 (1980).

Chapter 10

1. Michael Krausz, "Paths and Projects," *Limits of Rightness* (Lanham, Md.: Rowman and Littlefield Publishers, 2000), chap.13.
2. Ibid., p. 143–144.
3. Andreea Deciu Ritivoi, "Interpreting Historical Legacies: The Ethos of Transition in Eastern Europe," *Interpretation and its Objects: Studies in the Philosophy of Michael Krausz* Amsterdam: Rodopi Publishers, 2003), pp. 185–186.
4. Ibid., p. 186.
5. Louis Mink, "Narrative Form as a Cognitive Instrument," *The Writing of History: Literary Form and Historical Understanding*, eds. Robert H. Canary and Henry Kozicki (Madison: WI: University of Wisconsin Press, 1978), p. 152.
6. David Novitz, "Art, Narrative, and Human Nature," *Philosophy and Literature*, 13:1 (April 1989), p. 72; Roy Schafer, "Action and Narration in Psychoanalysis," *New Literary History* (1980), pp. 61–85; and Schafer, "Narration in the Psychoanalytic Dialogue," *Critical Inquiry* (Autumn 1980), p. 29–53.
7. Andreea Deciu Ritivoi, *Yesterday's Self: Nostalgia and the Immigrant Identity* (Lanham, Md.: Rowman & Littlefield Publishers, Inc., 2002).
8. Ritivoi, "Interpreting Historical Legacies," pp. 181–216; and Eva Hoffman, *Lost in Translation: A Life in a New Language* (New York: Penguin Books, 1994).
9. Novitz, "Art, Narrative, and Human Nature," p. 60.
10. Ibid., p. 61.
11. Ibid., p. 65.
12. Ibid., p. 62.
13. Ibid., p. 68.

14. Paul Thom, "Constituents of Interpretation," In Ritivoi, *Interpretation and its Objects*, p.116.

15. Krishna Roy, *Hermeneutics: East and West*, Jadavpur Studies in Philosophy, Second Series (Calcutta: Allied Publishers Ltd., 1993), p. 131.

16. Ibid., pp. 76–77.

17. Swami Vivekananda, *Practical Vedanta* (Calcutta: Mayavati, 1995), p. 18.

18. Ibid., p. 22.

19. Ibid., p. 25.

20. Ibid., p. 106.

21. Vibha Chaturvedi, "Reflections on the Interpretation of Religious Texts," In Ritivoi, *Interpretation and its Objects*, p. 308.

22. Karl Potter, *Presuppositions of India's Philosophies* (Englewood Cliffs, N.J.: Prentice-Hall, 1963); and S. R. Bhatt, *Vedic Wisdom, Cultural Inheritance and Contemporary Life* (Delhi: Sandeep Prekashan, 2004).

23. Ludwig Wittgenstein, *Culture and Value*, ed. G. H. von Wright, trans. Peter Winch (Oxford: Basil Blackwell, 1980), p. 46e, quoted in Chaturvedi, "Reflections on the Interpretation of Religious Texts," pp. 309–310, emphasis added.

24. Ibid., p. 310.

25. Ibid., p. 309.

26. Ibid., p. 307.

27. Courtenay Edward "Tom Brown" Stevens, Fellow of Magdalen College, Oxford, and former student of R. G. Collingwood, in personal conversation, 1969.

28. Arthur Danto, *Mysticism and Morality* (New York: Basic Books, 1972), esp. chap. 3.

29. John Dewey, *Art As Experience* (New York: Capricorn Books, 1934), esp. chap. 3; A. H. Maslow, *Religions, Values, and Peak Experiences* (New York: Viking Press, 1963), esp. chap. 3; Mihaly Czikszentmihalyi, *Flow: The Psychology of Optimal Experience* (New York: Harper and Row, 1990); and Bernard Berenson, *The Florentine Painters of the Renaissance* (New York: Putnam's Sons, 1912).

30. Danto, *Mysticism and Morality*, pp. 110–111.

31. Roberto Assogioli, *Psychosynthesis* (New York: Hobbs, Dorman & Co., 1965).

32. Chaturvedi, "Reflections on the Interpretation of Religious Texts," p. 308.

33. Ibid., 306.

34. Ibid.

35. Jill Stauffer, Fellow at Haverford College, correspondence with author, 15 November 2005.

36. John Kekes, *A Justification of Rationality* (Albany: State University of New York Press, 1976); and Bruce Hauptli, *The Reasonableness of Reason: Explaining Rationality Naturalistically* (Chicago, Ill.: Open Court, 1995).

37. Nelson Goodman, "The Way the World Is," reprinted Starmaking: Realism, Anti-Realism and Irrealism, ed. Peter McCormick (Cambridge, Mass.: MIT Press, 1996), p. 4.

38. Ken-ichi Sasaki, "Limits of Interpretation," in In Ritivoi, *Interpretation and its Objects*, p. 77.

BIBLIOGRAPHY

Ames, Roger, and Henry Rosemont, Jr. *The Analects of Confucius: A Philosophical Translation*. New York: Ballantine Books, 1999.

Assogioli, Roberto. Psychosynthesis. New York: Hobbs, Dorman & Co., 1965.

Beardsley, Monroe. "The Authority of the Text." In Iseminger. Intention and Interpretation.

Benedict, Ruth. The Chrysanthemum and the Sword: Patterns of Japanese Culture. New York and Scarborough: New American Library, 1974.

Berenson, Bernard. The Florentine Painters of the Renaissance. New York: Putnam's Sons, 1912.

Bhatt, S. R. Vedic Wisdom, Cultural Inheritance and Contemporary Life. Delhi: Sandeep Prekashan, 2004.

Brenner, H. P. "Introductory Appreciations." In Van Gogh in Perspective. Edited by Bogomila Welsh-Ovcharov. Englewood Cliffs, N.J.: Prentice Hall, 1974.

Chan, Wing-tsit. A Sourcebook in Chinese Philosophy. Princeton, N.J.: Princeton University Press, 1969.

Chapman, H. P. Rembrandt by Himself. Exhibition Catalogue. Glasgow Museums & Art Galleries, 1991.

Chaturvedi, Vibha. "Reflections on the Interpretation of Religious Texts." In Ritivoi. Interpretation and its Objects.

Chung-yuan, Chang. Creativity and Taoism: A Study of Chinese Philosophy, Art and Poetry. New York: Harper Colophon Books, 1970.

The Compact Oxford English Dictionary. 2nd ed. Oxford: Oxford University Press, 1996.

Cox, Christoph. "Versions, Dubs, and Remixes: Realism and Rightness in Aesthetic Interpretation." In Ritivoi. Interpretation and its Objects.

Crocker, David. "Interpretive Ideals and Truth Commissions." In Ritivoi. Interpretation and its Objects.

Czikszentmihalyi, Mihaly. Flow: The Psychology of Optimal Experience. New York: Harper and Row, 1990.

Danto, Arthur. Mysticism and Morality. New York: Basic Books, 1972.

Davidson, Donald. "On the Very Idea of a Conceptual Scheme." In Meiland and Krauz. Relativism.

Davies, Bronwyn, and Rom Harré. "Positioning: The Discursive Production of Selves," Journal of Theory and Social Behaviour, 20:1 (1990), pp. 43–63.

De Sousa, Ronald. "The Rationality of Emotions," Explaining Emotions. Edited by Amélie Oksenberg Rorty. Berkeley: University of California Press, 1980.

Dewey, John. Art as Experience. New York: Capricorn Books, 1934.

Findlay, J. N. "The Perspicuous and the Poignant." In Aesthetics. Edited by Harold Osborne. London: Oxford University Press, 1972.

Frankfurt, Harry. The Reasons of Love. Princeton, N.J.: Princeton University Press, 2004.

Fromm, Erich. To Have or To Be? New York: Harper and Row, 1976.

Gilot, F., and C. Lake. Life with Picasso. New York: McGraw-Hill, 1964.

Goodman, Nelson. "Just the Facts, Ma'am." In Krausz. Relativism: Interpretation and Confrontation.

————. "The Way the World Is." Reprinted in Starmaking: Realism, Anti-Realism and Irrealism. Edited by Peter McCormick. Cambridge, Mass.: MIT Press, 1996.

Graetz, H. R. The Symbolic Language of Vincent Van Gogh. New York: McGraw Hill, 1963.

Gupta, Chhanda. "Constructive Realism and the Question of Imputation." Krausz. Is There a Single Right Interpretation?

Hanna, Patricia, and Bernard Harrison. Word and World: Practice and the Foundations of Language. New York and Cambridge: Cambridge University Press, 2004.

Harré, Rom. "Is there a Basic Ontology for the Physical Sciences?" Dialectica, 51:1 (1997), pp. 17–33.

Harré Rom, and Michael Krausz. "Moral Relativism." In Varieties of Relativism. Oxford: Basil Blackwell, 1996.

Harrison, Bernard, and Patricia Hanna. "Interpretation and Ontology: Two Queries for Krausz." In Ritivoi. Interpretation and its Objects.

Hauptli, Bruce. The Reasonableness of Reason: Explaining Rationality Naturalistically. Chicago, Ill.: Open Court, 1995.

Hirsch, E. D. "In Defense of the Author." In Iseminger. Intention and Interpretation.

Hoffman, Eva. Lost in Translation: A Life in a New Language . New York: Penguin Books, 1994.

Iseminger, Gary, ed. Intention and Interpretation. Philadelphia, Penn.: Temple University Press, 1992.

Kandinsky, Wassily. Concerning the Spiritual in Art, and Painting in Particular. New York: Wittenborn, Schultz, 1963 [1921].

Kekes, John. A Justification of Rationality. Albany: State University of New York Press, 1976.

Krausz, Michael. "Creating and Becoming." In The Concept of Creativity in Science and Art. Edited by D. Dutton and M. Krausz. The Hague: Martinus Nijhoff Publishers, 1981.

————, ed. Relativism: Interpretation and Confrontation. Notre Dame, Ind.: Notre Dame University Press, 1989 and 1990.

————. Rightness and Reasons: Interpretation in Cultural Practices. Ithaca, N. Y.: Cornell University Press, 1993.

————. "Interpretation, Relativism, and Culture: Four Questions for Margolis." In Interpretation, Relativism and the Metaphysics of Culture: Themes in the Philosophy of Joseph Margolis. Edited by Michael Krausz and Richard Shusterman. Amherst, N.Y.: Humanity Press, 1999.

————. Limits of Rightness. Lanham, Md.: Rowman and Littlefield Publishers, 2000.

————. "Paths and Projects." In Limits of Rightness.

————, ed. Is there a Single Right Interpretation? University Park: Pennsylvania State University Press, 2002.

———— and Richard Shusterman, eds. Interpretation, Relativism, and the Metaphysics of Culture: Themes in the Philosophy of Joseph Margolis. Amherst, N.Y.: Humanity Press, 1999.

Lamarque, Peter. "Appreciation and Literary Interpretation." In Krausz. Is there a Single Right Interpretation?

————. "Objects of Interpretation," Metaphilosophy, 31:1/2 (January 2000), pp. 96–124.

————. "Object, Works, and Interpretation." In McKenna. Interpretation and Culture: Themes in the Philosophy of Michael Krausz, pp. 1–7.

Lau, D. C. Confucius: The Analects. London: Penguin, 1979.

Lopez-Pedraza, Rafael. Anselm Kiefer: After the Catastrophe. London, Thames and Hudson, 1996.

Lubin, Albert. Stranger on the Earth: A Psychological Biography of Vincent Van Gogh. New York: Holt, Rinehart, and Winston, 1972.

MacIntyre, Alasdair. "Relativism, Power, and Philosophy." In Krausz. Relativism: Interpretation and Confrontation.

Margolis, Joseph. Art and Philosophy. Brighton, UK: Harvester University Press, 1980.

————. "Robust Relativism." In Iseminger. Intention and Interpretation.

————."The Truth About Relativism," In Krausz. Relativism: Interpretation and Confrontation.

Maslow, A. H. Religions, Values, and Peak Experiences. New York: Viking Press, 1963.

Maxwell, Nicholas. "Art as its Own Interpretation." In Ritivoi. Interpretation and its Objects.

McDowell, John. "Scheme-Content Dualism and Empiricism." In The Philosophy of Donald Davidson. Library of Living Philosophers. Vol. 27. Edited by Lewis Edwin Hahn. Chicago and LaSalle Illinois: Open Court, 1999.

McKenna, Michael, ed. Interpretation and Culture: Themes in the Philosophy of Michael Krausz, special issue. Philosophy in the Contemporary World, 12:1 (Spring–Summer 2005).

————. "A Metaphysics for Krausz.." In Ritivoi. Interpretation and its Objects.

Meiland, Jack, and Michael Krausz, eds. Relativism: Cognitive and Moral. Notre Dame, Ind.: Notre Dame University Press, 1982.

Mink, Louis O. "Narrative Form as a Cognitive Instrument." In The Writing of History: Literary Form and Historical Understanding. Edited by Robert H. Canary and Henry Kozicki. Madison: University of Wisconsin Press, 1978.

Mohanty, Jitendra. "Phenomenological Rationality and the Overcoming of Relativism." In Krausz. Relativism: Interpretation and Confrontation.

Moore, Ronald. "Interpretive Ideals and Life Projects." In Ritivoi. Interpretation and its Objects.

Mukherji, Nirmalangshu. "Is There a General Notion of Interpretation?" In Ritivoi. Interpretation and its Objects.

Nehamas, Alexander. "The Postulated Author: Critical Monism as a Regulative Ideal," Critical Inquiry, 8 (Autumn 1981), 133–149.

Norton, David L. Imagination, Understanding, and the Virtue of Liberality. Lanham, Md., 1996.

Novitz, David. "Against Critical Pluralism." In Krausz, Is There a Single Right Interpretation? pp.101–121.

————. "Art, Narrative, and Human Nature," Philosophy and Literature, 13:1 (April 1989), pp. 57–74.

————. "Against Critical Pluralism." In Krausz. Is There a Single Right Interpretation?

Osmond, Susan Fegley. "Rembrandt's Self-Portraits," The World & I (September Issue, January 2000), pp. 2–14.

Pollock, Griselda. "Van Gogh and the Poor Slaves: Images of Rural Labor as Modern Art," Art History, 11 (September 1988), pp. 406–409.

Putnam, Hilary. "Truth and Convention: On Davidson's Refutation of Conceptual Relativism." In Krausz. Relativism: Interpretation and Confrontation.

Popper, Karl. "The Myth of the Framework." In The Abdication of Philosophy and the Public Good. 1st ed. Chicago, Ill.: Open Court Publishing Company, 1976.

Popper, Karl, and John C. Eccles. The Self and Its Brain: An Argument for Interactionism. London: Routledge & Kegan Paul, 1983.

Potter, Karl. Presuppositions of India's Philosophies. Englewood Cliffs, N.J.: Prentice-Hall, 1963.

Ritivoi, Andreea Deciu, ed. Interpretation and its Objects: Studies in the Philosophy of Michael Krausz. Amsterdam: Rodopi Publishers, 2003.

———. "Interpreting Historical Legacies: The Ethos of Transition in Eastern Europe." In Ritivoi. Interpretation and its Objects.

———. Yesterday's Self: Nostalgia and the Immigrant Identity. Lanham, Md.: Rowman & Littlefield Publishers, Inc., 2002.

Rosenberg, Harold. "The American Action Painters," Art News, 51 (1952), pp. 22–23, 48.

Roy, Krishna. Hermeneutics: East and West, Jadavpur Studies in Philosophy. Second Series. Calcutta: Allied Publishers Ltd., 1993.

Saltzman, Lisa. Anselm Kiefer and Art after Auschwitz. Cambridge, UK: Cambridge University Press, 1999.

Sasaki, Ken-ichi. "Limits of Interpretation." In Ritivoi. Interpretation and its Objects.

Schafer, Roy. "Action and Narration in Psychoanalysis," New Literary History, 12: 61–85 (1980), pp. 61–85.

———. "Narration in the Psychoanalytic Dialogue," Critical Inquiry (Autumn 1980), pp. 29–53.

Richard Shiff. "Through a Slow Medium," In Sultan. Chuck Close Prints.

Steinberg, Leo. Leonardo's Incessant Last Supper. New York: Zone Books, 2002.

Sultan, Terrie, ed. Chuck Close Prints: Process and Collaboration. Princeton, N.J.: Princeton University Press, 2003.

Taylor, Charles. Sources of the Self: The Making of Modern Identity. Cambridge, Mass.: Harvard University Press, 1980.

Thom, Paul. "Constituents of Interpretation." In Ritivoi. Interpretation and its Objects.

Nancy Weston. "Rightness, Ontology, and the Adjudication of Truth: Adumbrations from the Law's Trial." In Ritivoi. Interpretation and its Objects.

Van De Wetering, Ernst. "The Various Functions of Rembrandt's Self-portraits." In Rembrandt's Hidden Self-Portraits. Amsterdam: Museum Het Rembrandthuis, 2003.

Vivekananda, Swami. Practical Vedanta. Calcutta: Mayavati, 1995.

Waley, Arthur. The Analects of Confucius. New York: Vintage Books, 1989.

Weitz, Morris. "The Role of Theory in Aesthetics," Journal of Aesthetics and Art Criticism, 15 (1956), pp. 27–35.

Whorf, Benjamin Lee. Language, Thought, and Realty. New York: Technology Press of MIT and John Wiley & Sons, Inc., 1962.

Ludwig Wittgenstein. Culture and Value. Edited by G. H. von Wright. Translated by Peter Winch. Oxford: Basil Blackwell, 1980.

ABOUT THE AUTHOR

Michael Krausz is the Milton C. Nahm Professor of Philosophy at Bryn Mawr College. His publications include *Rightness and Reasons: Interpretation in Cultural Practices*, *Limits of Rightness*, *Varieties of Relativism* (with Rom Harré), and *Interpretation and Transformation: Explorations in Art and the Self.* As well, Krausz is contributor to and editor of nine volumes on such topics as Relativism, Rationality, Interpretation, Cultural Identity, Metaphysics of Culture, Creativity, Interpretation of Music, and the Philosophy of R. G. Collingwood. A Festschrift dedicated to his philosophical work, *Interpretation and its Objects: Studies in the Philosophy of Michael Krausz*, edited by Andreea Ritivoi, was published in 2003. He is cofounder of the Greater Philadelphia Philosophy Consortium. As a visual artist, Krausz has had twenty solo exhibitions in galleries in the United States and abroad. He is also the Artistic Director and Conductor of the Great Hall Chamber Orchestra at Bryn Mawr.

INDEX

abrogation, 113
Absolute, the, 109, 110, 113, 114, 118, 120
absolutis(m)(ts), 58, 59, 63, 114
accountability, 31, 120
accuracy, 24, 25, 78
act(ion)(s), 29, 31–33, 61, 64, 85, 91,
    97, 98, 104, 105
Action Painters, American, 98
activit(ies)(y), 1, 2, 37
    artistic/creative a., 100, 101
    elucidatory a., 3, 4
    intentional a., 118
    interpretive a., 1, 4, 7, 11, 43–46, 50,
        52, 64, 71, 103, 105, 106, 108,
        113, 115, 119, 121
    praxial a., 76, 78
actual, the, 103
actualit(ies)(y), 90, 91, 103
adjudication, 33, 59
admissibility, 4, 12, 30, 35, 41, 89, 103, 119
    ideal a., 22
Advaita Vedantic doctrine, 109
aestheticist tradition, 18
Aatma, 110. *See also* One
affection, 93
agreement(s), 26, 29, 39, 65, 71, 79
    disagreement, 36, 38, 39
aims, 2–4, 7, 30, 41, 105, 120
    edificatory and elucidatory a., 108,
        110, 115
Aldrich, Virgil, 42
All, 109
allusiveness, 119
alternativity, 66
    a. argument, Davidson's, 65, 66
anachronism, 10
Analects (Confucius), 67
analogue, 52, 62
analysis, 39
anarchy, 11
anger, 85–89, 94
answers, 14, 15, 17, 28, 32, 43, 44, 120, 121
    single vs. multiple right a., 31, 50

shifting a., 91
    unique a., 26
anthropologist, bi-cultural/bi-lingual, 61
appropriateness, 13, 18, 29, 85, 86, 89
aptness, 13
arbitrariness, 50, 51, 59, 79
Aristarchus, 54
arithmetic, 14
art(ist)(work)(s), 1, 9, 10, 15–17, 20, 42,
    44–46, 53, 73, 97–101, 106, 112
    a.-aesthetic expression, 101
    Chinese a., 100
    a. exhibitions, 93
    a. historian, 19
    a. vs. life, 98
    modern a., 100
    private a., 42
    a. world, 18
artifacts, 72, 73, 75
    artifactual domain, 75
artistic program, 93
aspection, 42
assertion(s), 4, 108, 110, 111, 119. *See*
    also elucidation
    Harrison and Hanna's a., 80
    multiplist a., 24
    a. of Oneness, 120
astonishment, 80
at-homeness, 93
atonement, 100, 101
at-oneness, 86, 92, 93, 100, 101
attachment, possessive, 93
attainment, 100
attention, 10, 13, 19, 39, 87, 90, 97
    inattention, 90
attitude(s), 1, 4, 32, 85, 91, 98, 110, 111
    a. of assertion, 110
    intentional a., 115–118
    multiplist a., 30, 31
    transformative a., 99
automobiles, 74
awareness, 117, 120

bab(ies)(y), 16, 75
bankruptcy, 89
beauty, 101
behavior, 88
  appropriate b., 41
  child's misbehavior, 87
  good b., 61, 64
  moral b., 63
Being, 114
being, state of, 10, 100
beings, 82, 118
  inherent b., 104
  realized b., 114
belief(s), 2, 3, 27, 52, 58, 59, 65, 87,
      104, 105, 108, 110
  assertoric b., 111
  false b., 58
  religious b., 110, 111
Benedict, Ruth, 61, 64, 67
betrayal, 19–21
Betrayal Interpretation, 20. *See also*
      interpretation(s)
beyondness, 115, 120
bivalence, 11, 13
bivalent logic, 11, 13, 14
bivalent values, 13
blasphemy, 114
bliss, 94, 104, 114, 116, 117, 119
book(s), 28, 80–82, 87, 98
botanists, 74
Braque, George, 99
Broyer, John Albin, 100, 101
Buddhis(m)(ts), 86, 93, 94, 112
  B. community, 86
  B. monks, 16
  Tibetan B., 93
  B. view of emotions, 93, 94
Buddhist Dialectics, Institute for, 86
Butterfield, Andrew, 20
by-product, 100

calculation, 10, 14
cancellations, symmetry of, 20
canvass(es), 75, 92, 93, 97
career, 8, 100

categor(ies)(y), 1, 57, 62, 72, 115
  constructed c., 74
  c. mistake, 103, 108
Catholics, 29
Central Park of New York City, 16
change(s), 3, 87, 100, 104
  c. of belief, 87
  counterchange, 20
  c. in identity, 27
  impending c., 98
  c. of reference frame, 27
Chapman, H. P., 8, 9
character, 53
  grammatical c., 66
  moral c., 66
characters, 7, 73, 90
Chaturvedi, Vibha, 35, 36, 38, 39, 109–
      111, 115, 116
chemical composition, 44, 52
Chinese (language), 66, 68
Chinese (people), 85
Christ, 19
Christo, 1, 16, 17
  Gates, 1, 16–18
Chung-yuan, Chang, 100, 101
circumference, 24, 25
claim(s), 11, 13, 21, 24, 26, 29, 31, 32,
      46, 52, 54, 60, 68, 72, 77, 110
  c. to admissibility, 89
  assertable c., 74
  cognitive c., 110
  competing/contending c., 58, 121
  conceptually structured c., 78
  contradictory c., 13
  distributive c., 58, 72
  dual c., 27
  epistemic c., 73, 82
  false c., 2, 3, 108
  identity c., 114
  multiplist c., 59
  ontic c., 73
  c. to rightness, 32
  truth-c., 82, 91
  c. to universal validity, 116
  value c., 57

clock(s), 14, 15
Close, Chuck, 1, 53, 54
   John, 1, 53
closure, 30, 31, 89, 90
co-creation, 15
cognate(s), 2, 55, 57, 68, 69
collection(s), 7, 8
   ultimate c., 81
color(s), 17, 53, 72, 99
commitment(s), 18, 71
   intellectual c., 92
   moral c., 111
   realist c., 73
   vocational c., 92
Commodity Interpretation, 9, 10. *See*
   also interpretation(s)
concept(ion)(s), 52, 63, 65, 67, 77, 82,
   91, 110, 119
   governing c., 71
   limiting c., 22
   specular c., 76
conceptual schem(as)(es), 55, 57, 60,
   62–66, 68, 69, 73, 74
   alternative c. s., 65, 68
   home c. s., 68
concern, 82, 86, 87, 89, 109
concession, 107
   constructivist c., 73
conclusiveness, 31–33, 59
condition(s), 9, 15, 38, 93
   boundary c., 57
   cultural c., 43
   c. of displaced italics, 19
   identity c., 27, 29, 43, 72, 73, 75, 103,
     110, 116, 121
   individuating c., 120
   ineliminable c., 30
   interim c., 30
   interpretive c., 22
   intersubjectively sharable c., 120
   many-to-many c., 94
   multiplist c., 7, 8, 11, 12, 15, 16, 18,
     21, 23, 24, 26–30, 33, 37, 43,
     71, 75, 79, 81, 121
   supermultiplist c., 19

necessary c., 12, 65
c. of non-duality, 100
pluralist c., 81
positive c., 94
singularist c., 7, 8, 11, 12, 15, 16, 20,
   21, 23, 26, 28, 35, 37, 75
sufficient c., 66
three-term c., 14
confirmation, 120
conflict of interest(s), 50
Confucius, 67
   Analects, 67
congruous (the term), 14
consciousness, 97, 108, 109, 115, 117,
   118, 120
   self-c., 8
consideration(s), 2, 22, 85, 105
   extra-scheme c., 58
   meta-c., 21
   summing up c., 90
consol(ation)(ers), 2, 3, 108, 113, 114
   conflict between c. and under-
     standing, 3
   false c., 3
constellations, 57
constituents, 81
constraints, 13, 31, 68, 107
   c. of language, 120
construction(ist)(s), 45, 73, 78, 104–
   narrative c., 90, 106
constructive realism. *See* realism,
   constructive
constructivis(m)(ts), 71–76
consummation, 99
   aesthetic c., 101
content, 20, 57, 62
   assertoric c., 109
context(s), 11, 12, 42, 67
   aesthetic c., 45
   historical c., 7
   religious c., 111, 116
contradiction, 9, 10, 14, 20, 60, 87
contrariness, 20, 110
contrast, 25, 64
conundrum, 110

convention(s), 15, 42, 73, 74
conventionality, 115
conversation, 98
Copernican system, 54
Copernicus, 54
countability, 12
Cox, Cristoph, 45–47
critical monism. *See also* singularism
critical pluralism, 37
critics, 18, 44
Crocker, David, 12, 35–37
cultural realm, 53, 75
culture(s), 1, 27, 33, 38, 62, 66, 75, 116
    alternative c., 66
    guilt/shame c., 61, 64, 66–68
    Mexican and American c., 57
    Tibetan c., 85
Czikszentmihalyi, Mihaly, 112

Da Vinci, Leonardo, 1, 19
    Last Supper, 1, 19, 21
Dalai Lama. *See* Gyatso, Tenzin
Danto, Arthur, 43, 112
Davidson, Donald, 55, 57, 58, 60, 62–
    66, 68, 69
Davies, Bronwyn, 91
de Jongh, Eddy, 9
De Sousa, Ronald, 86, 87, 89, 91
death, 2, 3, 8, 88,
    bodily d. 112
    deathless, 109
    ultimate d., 111
decisiveness, 32, 33
deconstruction, 46, 115, 119
defendant, 31
definition, 7, 58, 90, 101
    self-d., 8
deformation, 46
DeKooning, Willem, 98
delight, 87, 94
deliverances, 62
demarcation, 75
demonstration, 86, 99, 119
Derrida, Jacques, 45
description(s), 60, 72, 74, 76, 79–81,

    89, 90, 119
desire, 32
determinability, 32
determination, 22, 33
    d. of law, 31
    truth-d., 78
development, artistic, 98–101
Dewey, John, 98–100, 112
Dharamsala, India, 86
Dialectics, Buddhist, 86
difference(s), 23, 28, 29, 75, 111
    practical d., 33, 35
dimension(s), 2, 94
    political d., 106
    theological d., 19
disagreement(s), 36, 38, 39
disciples, 19
discourse, 27, 41, 57, 73, 82, 91, 107
disinterest, 3, 90
disparities, 66
disposition, 31, 32, 53, 90, 97
distinction(s), 2, 7, 21, 22, 33, 35–37,
    44–47, 65, 75, 78, 98, 100, 101,
    105, 114, 115, 118 120
    tripartite d., 76
diversion, 107
diversity, 12, 39, 109, 111, 115, 116
    cultural d., 58
    historical d., 58
doubt(s), 54, 92
drawing(s), 10, 88
dream, 33
dualism(s), 2, 108, 113, 115, 118, 120
dualit(ies)(y), 115, 119, 120
    non-d., 116
    subject-object d., 116, 119, 120
dumpsite, 16

edification, 2–4, 108, 110, 111, 115
ego-form, 100
ego-self, 86, 120
elucidation, 2–4, 30, 103, 108, 110,
    111, 115
embeddedness, 50, 72
embodiment, 44, 109, 112, 116, 117, 120

emotion(s), 1, 85–90, 92–95
English, 42, 60, 61, 66, 67, 68
   British E., 61
   ordinary E., 93
enigma, 110
entit(ies)(y), 60, 61, 74, 76, 80
   cultural e., 1, 27
   daughter/mother e., 27
   fictional acting e., 62, 64
   higher order e., 81
   linguistic e., 82
epiphanic episode, 98
episodes, 104
epistemic lack, 12
epistemic matter, 18
equipoise, 115
equivalencies, lexical, 67
etching(s), 10, 43
ethics, Greek, 67
   e. stance, 33
Eucharist, 20
Eucharist Interpretation, 20, 21. *See
   also* interpretation(s)
event(s), 31, 90, 91, 99, 100, 105, 107
   contradictory e., 101
   imaginary e., 106
   opposing e., 104
   public e., 16–18
evidence, 30, 111
exaltation, spiritual, 100
exhibition(s), 93, 97, 99
existence, 43, 44, 46, 54, 58, 78, 100
   artist's e., 98
   conventional e., 112, 115
   inherent e., 112, 121
   non-e. of common logical framework, 54
   personal e., 107
   pre-e., 64
   e. of prenarrative facts, 72
   e. of transcendental objects, 71
experience(r)(s), 42, 62, 63, 72, 82, 89,
   92, 98, 99
   bliss-like (flow-like) e., p. 19
   dualistic e., 97
   epiphenic e., 97

   inner e., 108
   e. as intentional attitude, 115
   lived e., 104, 112
   ontological e., 100
   peak e., 97, 112
   personal e., 1
   putative e., 121
   e. of realization, 115
   religious e., 1, 101, 112, 116
explanandum, 44
explanans, 44
expressiveness, 7
eye(s), 17, 53
   God's eye view, 22
   invariant e., 53

fabrication, 73
fact of the matter, 63, 64, 91, 105, 113
   praxial f. of m., 28, 29
facts, 29, 72, 87, 90, 91, 107
faculties, 92, 98
fairness, 94
fallibilism, 59
falsification, 109, 114
falsity, 13, 76, 78, 82, 119, 120
fear, 85, 86, 92, 112
features, 7, 18, 20, 36, 41, 43, 51–53, 58,
   73, 77, 81, 87, 94, 105, 118
   common f., 15
   emergent f., 99
   incongruent f., 106
   f. of intentional phenomena, 41
   f. of interpreters, 1
   f. of interpretive activity, 1
   salient f., 19, 86
Fleisher Art Memorial, Samuel S., 17
flourishing, 2, 4
flower(s), 12, 92
foot-lengths, 25
force, 19, 32, 61, 115
   f. of transformation, 46
form(s), 21, 62, 63, 97
   ego-f., 100
   logical f., 76
   objectified f., 117

Foucault, Michel, 45
frame(s). *See* reference frame(s)
framelessness, 114
frame-relativity, 41, 42, 51, 53, 114
framework, 54, 60, 104
    alternative f., 66
    conceptual f., 43
    f. of knowing, 80
    linguistic f., 57
    logical f., 54
freedom, 112, 117, 120
friend(s), 49, 86–93, 97, 99
funeral, 87 88
future, 104, 106

game, 1, 41, 98, 106
Ganges River, 16
Gates (Christo and Jean-Claude), 1, 16–18
geocentric system, 54
Germans, 8, 85, 86
Gestalt switch, 54
goals, 2, 59, 108
God's eye point of view, 22
Goethe, Johann Wolfgang von, 19
Goodman, Nelson, 38, 45, 49, 73–75, 119
goodness, 67
gratitude, 86–88
grounds, 30–33, 35, 37, 39, 44, 45, 65,
        66, 71. *See* also evidence
guilt, 61, 64
 g. culture, 64, 67
        American, 61
        g. vs. shame c., 64, 66
Gupta, Chhanda, 51, 52
guru-teacher, 116

Hamlet (Shakespeare), 71, 73
Hanna, Patricia, 11, 23–27, 29, 33, 37,
        64, 71, 72, 74–80
Harré, Rom, 91
Harrison, Bernard, 11, 23, 26, 27, 29,
        33, 37, 64, 71, 72, 74–79, 82
Head Transformation (Samaras), 1, 53
healing, 2, 30
Henri, Robert, 100

Hill, Miriam, 17
Hindus, 29
historian(s), 44
    art h., 19
    Marxist h., 10
history, 4, 9, 85, 86, 106
    German/Nazi h., 8
hope, 2, 3, 108
Hopi, 61, 63, 64, 68
hour(s), 14, 49
human nature, 58, 91
humanity, 9, 67
hypothesis, scientific, 111

ideal(ism)(s), 7, 11, 22, 27, 77, 79
    generally defined i., 38
    interpretive (of interpretation), 33, 79
    multiplist/singularist i., 30, 35
identity, 16, 27–29, 41, 44, 49, 50, 60,
        75, 80, 81
    i. claim, 114
    i.-formation, 8–10
    i. independent of reference frame, 113
    narrative i., 106
    numeral/numerical i., 16, 24
    praxial i., 28
    self-i., 104
    i. between *tvad* and *tad*, 108
    work-i., 43, 51
identity conditions, 27, 29, 43, 72, 73,
        103, 110, 116, 121
Identity Formation Interpretation, 8–10.
        See also interpretation(s)
image(s), 8, 53, 62
improvement, spiritual, 2
imputation, 49–51, 53, 55
inches, 23–25, 27, 28, 37, 77
incommensurability, 38, 54
incompatibility, 20, 23, 54, 87
inconclusivity, 30, 31
incongruence, 9, 13–16, 19, 21, 24, 110
    internal i., 20
    mutual i., 20
indecision, 33
indifference, 88

individuals, 3, 62, 72–75, 93, 104, 105, 115, 117
individuality, 105, 107, 112, 117
individuation, 28
    praxial i., 29
Indo-Europeans, 61, 64
inquiry, 12, 13, 22, 29, 30, 33, 41, 52, 59, 76
    constative i., 58
    ontological i., 78, 82
insincerity, 110
institution(s), 20, 30, 31, 67, 76, 77, 78
italics, condition of displaced, 19
intentionalit(ies)(y), 41–47 *passim*, 118
    Paradox of i., 115
interests, 1, 9, 15, 18, 19, 22, 24, 25, 28, 33, 36–38, 50, 74, 79–81, 89, 95, 106, 110
    opposing i., 49
    selfish i., 93
interfusion, 100
interlocutor, 29, 36, 38
interpretability, 103
    multiple i., 8, 20
    Paradox of i., 113
    uni., 103
interpretandum, 44
interpretans, 44
interpretation, 1, 2, 15–18, 22, 28, 30, 31, 36, 38, 43, 44, 46, 49–51, 53, 54, 71, 81, 105, 114, 116. *See also* Betrayal Interpretation, Commodity Interpretation, Eucharist Interpretation, Identity Formation Interpretation,
    adjunct i., 15, 44
    admissible/inadmissible i., 7, 9, 11–14, 19, 20, 23, 26, 27, 29, 30, 32, 33, 35–38, 44, 49, 50, 59, 71, 73, 91, 103
    aim of i., 2–4, 7, 10
    alternative i., 11, 12, 37
    competing (contending/opposing) i., 2, 11, 13, 15, 27, 35, 59, 111
    comprehensive i., 19–21

conclusive/inc. i., 32, 33
core (reflexive) i., 44
dumpsite i., 16
exorcist i., 8
false/true i., 11, 12, 42
formalist i., 7
holy site i., 16
hyphenated i., 20
ideals of i., 7, 79, *see also* multiplism, singularism
incongru(ent)(ous) i., 7–9, 13–15, 19, 21
individuating between i., 20
interaction between i., 19
interpretations of i., 44–46
intra-religious differences between i., 111
limits of i., 82, 120, 121
Marxist-feminist i., 7
multiplist/singularist i., 20, 43, 45, 50, 82
musical i., 15
objects of i., 2, 7–9, 11, 15, 16, 18–20, 22–24, 26–29, 33, 39, 41–43, 45, 46, 49–51, 71, 72, 77–81, 103, 110, 116, 119, 121
    o. of i. vs. i., 7, 8, 44–46, 51, 115
    single vs. collection of o. of i., 7
overaching i., 21
preferred i., 35, 36, 59
psychological i., 7
right i., 29, 72
something beyond i., 103
i.-text, 46
i. theori(es)(sts), 7, 71
valid i., 20
interpreter(s), 1, 2, 4, 8, 9, 15, 17, 18, 39, 42, 45, 67, 68, 85, 108, 109, 116
interpretive activity, 1, 2, 4, 7, 11, 43–46, 50–52, 64, 71, 103, 105, 106, 108, 113, 115, 119, 121
intervention, 21
intolerance, 13
invention(s), 20, 78
investigation, 82

Jacobson, Thora, 17
Japanese style, 53
jealousy, 86, 93
Jean-Claude, 1
  Gates, 1, 16–18
John (Close), 1, 53
joint(s), 73–75, 81
joy, 86–88, 92, 94, 117
judge(s), 31, 32
judgment(s), 1, 4, 11, 89, 91, 116
  admissible j., 13
  singular j., 31
jury, 31

Kandinsky, Wassily, 97
Kant, Immanuel, 1, 82
Kiefer, Anselm, 8, 11
  Shulamith, 8
kindness, 8
Kline, Franz, 98
knowledge, 2, 3, 42, 58, 59, 67, 72, 103,
     108, 121
  conceptual k., 82
  dualistic k., 115
  false k., 109
  unknown k., 90
kosher, practice of, 4, 37
Krasner, Lee, 98
Krausz, Michael, 35, 43, 100, 101
  Limits of Rightness, 7, 79
Kuhn, Thomas, 54

labor, 7
  artistic l., 112
Lamarque, Peter, 19, 43, 44, 50, 51
language(s), 57, 62, 63, 65–68, 74, 77,
     78, 91, 119, 120
  European l., 61, 68
  foreign l., 60
  home l., 67
  Hopi l., 61, 68
  meta-l., 60
  natural l., 66
  object l., 60
  private l., 42

religious l., 111
Last Supper (Da Vinci), 1, 19, 21
layering, 42, 72, 73
length, 1, 23, 25, 28, 77
level(s), 22, 24, 27, 43, 44, 90
  absolute l., 120
  l. of consciousness, 109, 120
  conventional l., 113, 115, 120
  l. of description, 80–82
  meta-l., 21, 22
  object l., 22
  primitive l., 73, 74
  l.-relative, 21
  sub-atomic l., 80
  super-l., 22
life, 4, 57, 74, 80, 90, 91, 107, 109
  artist's l., 98
  l. of believer, 111
  l. after death, 112
  fragmentation of l., 101
  lifeless, 98
  l. programs, 97
  ultimate aim of l., 115
Limits of Rightness (Krausz), 7, 79
litigants, 32
location, 86, 104, 115
  cultural l., 1
logic(s), 9, 110
  bivalent l., 11, 13, 14
  l. of motivation, 104
  multivalent l., 11, 13
loss of individuality, 112
love(rs), 67, 86, 93, 94, 116, 117, 120
  l. of God, 117

MacIntyre, Alasdair, 59, 66–68
mankind, 63
mantra, 1, 105, 108–110, 114, 115, 119,
     120
map(s), schematic, 97
Margolis, Joseph, 11, 13, 14, 50, 51, 58
Maslow, Abraham, 97, 112
metalanguage, 60
matrix(es), 41, 63
Maxwell, Nicholas, 15, 18–21, 44, 45

McCleodganj, India, 86
McDowell, John, 62
McKenna, Michael, 72–76
meaning, 4, 20, 21, 41, 68, 77–79, 81,
   91, 112
   essentialist m., 1
   multiple m., 42
   religious m., 101
meaningfulness, 58
measurement, 23, 25, 37, 77–79, 100
mediator, singularist/multiplist, 29, 30
memories, 8
metaphors, 62
Metropolitan Museum, 53
microns, 23–25, 27, 28, 37, 77
middle, excluded, 13
Mink, Louis , 90, 91, 105–107
minute(s), 14
misdeed, 61
misgivings, 29, 68
mixedness, 88
models, 9, 13, 15, 24, 46, 87–89, 92, 94,
   95, 97
modul(i)(us), 14, 23, 26, 33, 77
Mohanty, Jitendra, 42
molecules, 64, 80
moment(s), 19, 20, 88, 89, 92, 98, 100,
   112, 118
monetary system, 41
monks, 16
monism. *See* critical monism
Moore, Ronald, 41, 42, 81
Morgenbesser, Sidney, 81
Moslems, 29
motivation, 9, 104, 112, 113
   Paradox of M., 111
movement, 88, 113, 114, 117, 118
Mukherji, Nirmalangshu, 1
multiplicity, 18, 33, 50, 67, 81, 89, 100, 109
multiplis(m)(ts), 7, 12, 13, 19, 30, 31,
   59, 75, 76, 78, 115
   m. condition(s), 7, 8, 11, 12, 15, 16,
      18, 21, 23, 24, 26–30, 33, 37,
      43, 71, 75, 80–82, 121; *see also*
      condition(s)

supermultiplist c., 19
   m. vs. singularism, 7–11 *passim*, 23–
      33 *passim*, 35–39 *passim*
Munz, James, 101
musical scores, 1
Muti, Riccardo, 16
mysticism, 119
"The Myth of the Framework" (Popper), 54
mythology, personal, 90, 97, 100, 101

narrative, 3, 20, 72, 89–93, 95, 104, 107
   congruent n., 90, 107
   incoherent n., 105
   religious n., 92
   self-n., 105, 106
narrativity, 107, 113
nature, 1, 7, 61, 62, 64, 73, 76
Nazi sites, 8
neo-Nazi, 8
Neurath, Otto, 73
Nietzsche, Friedrich, 45
nonbeliever, 111
noun, 1
Novitz, David, 11, 42, 72, 106, 107

object(s) of interpretation, 1, 2, 7–9, 11,
      12, 15, 16, 18–20, 22–24, 26–29,
      33, 36, 39, 41–46, 49–51, 71, 80,
      81, 103, 110, 119–121
objecthood, 117
objectification, 28, 73
occasions, 4, 16, 24
One, 109–111, 113–115, 118–120
ontolog(ies)(y), 63, 71, 72, 78, 79
open-endedness, 21, 44, 81
opinion(s), 36, 38, 63, 110
opportunities, 99
opposition, 13, 100, 119
oppression, 13
Osmond, Susan Fegley, 9
other(s), 12, 38, 65, 91, 101, 104, 105
outcomes, 36, 77, 78
Oxford English Dictionary, 2, 14

painting(s), 7, 8, 10, 17, 19, 20, 24, 41,
    43, 44, 79, 97
  act-p., 98
  cubist p., 99
  Tao-p., 100
paradigms, 57
paradox(es), 103, 110–120 *passim*
  soteriological p., 109
paradoxicality, 115
Paradox of
  P. of Framing, 114, 115
  P. of Intentionality, 115–117
  P. of Interpretability, 113, 114
  P. of Motivation, 111, 113
  P. of Rationality, 118–120
  P. of Self-Recognition, 117, 118
  P. of Self-Reference, 110
  P. of Truth and Oneness, 120, 121
parent(s), 87, 93
particles, sub-atomic, 24, 80
passerby, Buddhist, 86, 93
past, 9, 90
  Germany's Nazi p., 8
  reconstructed p., 106
path(es), 86, 107, 113
  edificatory p., 110
  soteriological p., 15
pedestrians, 74
perception(s), 52, 119
  Gestalt p., 94
performance(s), 1, 73
periods, 62, 90
  Baroque p., 57
persona, 9
personal mythology. *See* mythology,
    personal
personal program. *See under* pro-
    gram(me)(s)
personhood, 67
perspectivism, 80
phenomen(a)(ology)(on), 2, 3, 19, 80–
    82, 110
  action p., 64
  antecedently present p., 64
  p. of death, 3

emergent p., 80
p. of human life, 74
intentional p., 41
p. of self-deception, 105
philosophers, 9, 101
physical items, 98
physical order, 1
physicists, 74
pipe, 99
pity, 86, 88, 89
plausibility, 13
pluralizing, 18, 45
Podro, Michael, 19–21
pointer, 67
polic(ies)(y), 91, 105, 106
political dimension, 106
Pollock, Jackson, 98
Popper, Karl, 54, 59, 60, 97
  "The Myth of the Framework, 54
portrait(s)(ure), 10
  self-p., 8–10, 14
  unintentional p. of our time, 17
possibilit(ies)(y), 2–4, 38, 39, 43, 46, 47,
    59, 66, 75, 79, 81, 88, 100, 101,
    107, 108, 114, 116, 120
  contradictory p., 20
post-Romantic period, 10
postulation, 33
The Potato Eaters (Van Gogh), 1, 7
potentialit(ies)(y), 103, 108
  antecedent p., 61
practices, 1, 4, 13, 22, 23, 26–28, 37,
    41, 42, 44, 50, 51, 57–59, 64,
    67, 74–79, 81
  p.-centered account of objects, 74
  determinative p., 79
  discursive p., 91
  interpretive p., 73
  linquistic p., 27, 76, 78, 79, 82
  meditative p., 105
  psychotherapeutic p., 105
  translation p., 68
praxial situations, 78
precision, 24, 25
predication, 51, 120

preferability, 35, 59
preference(s), 32, 37
preoccupation, 8, 53
presupposition(s), 4
  absolute p., 57
principles, contrary, 20
priorit(ies)(y), 88, 117
  logical p., 10
process(es), 1–3, 17, 46, 53, 58, 104, 113
  artistic/creative p., 99, 100
  p. of becoming, 99
  p. of identity formation, 8
  political p., 106
  p. of proof, 31
  p. of realization, 109, 120
  p. of social interaction, 91
product(ion)(s), 1, 53, 58, 91, 100
  art p., 46, 97, 99, 101
  by-p., 100
  p. of Enlightenment thought, 19
  p. of intentional acts, 41, 118
  p. of interpretive practices, 9, 73
  p. of narratives, 104
  p. of objectifications, 73
  p. of practices, 28
  p. of praxial activity, 76
  p. of reference frames, 78
program(me)(s), 2, 4, 41, 95, 97, 100, 101, 106, 107, 110
  artistic p., 93
  p. of edification without elucidation, 3
  p. for emotions, 93
  interpretive p., 8–11, 16, 28, 33, 51
  multiplist p., 14
  personal p., 2, 97, 100, 101, 106, 107
  p. for self-transformation, 105
project(s), 18, 24, 38, 42, 95
  constructive p., 46
  edificatory p., 4
  major long-term p., 87
  transformative p., 2
projection(ism), 49–53, 119
projectionist view, 51
propert(ies)(y), 19, 36, 43, 49, 51, 52, 54, 72, 81

  dimensional p., 26
  imputed p., 43, 50, 73
  microstructural p., 52
  non-trivial p., 49
  real p., 51, 52
  salient p., 53
  semantic p., 42
  transfer of p., 67
  work-p., 43
proposition(s), 3, 76–79, 120
  falsifiable p., 3
  truth of a p., 57
propriety of use, 24
Protestants, 29
prototype(s), 98
psychodrama, 20
psychotherapeutic practices, 105
Ptolemy, 54
purpose(s), 9, 15, 18, 19, 22, 24, 25, 28, 33, 36–38, 49, 50, 67, 72, 74, 79–81, 89, 91, 95, 106, 110
  analytic p., 87
  relativist p., 60
Purva-Mimamsa school, 39

quality, 17, 99
question beggingness, 119
questions , 21, 26, 28, 50, 67, 90, 92, 98, 113, 114
  q. of admissibility, 121
  constructionist q., 46
  unanswerable q., 120

rationa(ity)(le), 36, 37, 86, 92, 119
  Paradox of R., 118
reaction(s), 10, 61, 91, 105
realism, constructive (relative), 29, 71–77–80, 82
  Harrison and Hannah's c. r., 76, 77–79
  metaphysical r., 72, 74, 77
realit(ies)(y), 26, 31, 52, 62, 72–77, 82, 108, 111, 112
  objective r., 100
  ultimate r., 74, 109
  uninterpreted r., 63

realization, 1, 4, 88, 104, 107, 108, 113–115, 118, 120
  final r., 109, 115
  self-r., 2, 37, 98, 101, 105, 107–110, 117
reason(s), 7, 10, 14, 15, 18, 22, 26, 29, 31–33, 35–37, 50, 53, 59–61, 66, 79, 94, 105, 106, 119
  ampliative r., 36–38, 60
  determinative r., 36, 37
  epistemic r., 58
  political r., 33
reasonableness, 11, 13, 29, 30, 110
reciprocal counterchange, 20
recollection, 118
reconciliation, 30, 100, 101
refere(ee)(nt), 77
reference frame(s), 9, 11, 14–18, 22–29, 33, 37, 38, 41–43, 49–55, 57, 69, 71–74, 76, 79–82, 85–92, 94, 95, 103–106, 110, 113, 114, 118, 119
  admissible r. f., 50
  r. f. embeddedness, 50
  incongruent r. f., 85, 106
  interpreter's r. f., 17
  non-absolute (conventional) r. f., 110, 114, 118
reflexive thesis, 44
refuge, 109, 115
reinterpretation, 27
relation(ship)(s), 7, 8, 14, 15, 39, 41, 51, 52, 54, 60, 62, 77, 80, 85, 86, 90, 93, 103, 104, 106, 110, 113–115, 118
  color r., 99
  human r., 98
  r. among languages, 67
  logical r., 54
  positive r., 93
  selfish r., 93
  symbiotic r., 2
relationist view, Gupta's, 52
relativis(m)(ts), 13, 57–65, 67–69
  anti-r., 58
  non-r., 60

robust r., 58
strident r., 79
relevance, 15, 104
relief, 32, 86–88
Rembrandt van Rijn, 1, 8–11, 14
representative cases, 1
resentment, 89
residue, 14, 23
resolution, 31, 32, 90, 107
response(s), 27, 43, 88, 90
  absolutist r., 64
  emotional r., 86, 93
  irrational r., 91, 105
riddle, 110
right(ness), 31, 32, 36, 42, 57–60, 68, 103, 121
rights, property, 67
Ritivoi, Andreea Deciu, 32, 104
rituals, communal, 17
river, 16
Rorty, Richard, 45
Rosenberg, Harold, 98
Roy, Krishna, 108
rules, 41, 60
sacramental component, 20
Saddhus, 16
salience(s), 1, 19, 36, 41, 52–54
Samaras, Lucas, 1, 53
  Head Transformation, 1, 53
same-aims-proviso, 2
sameness, 27, 29, 39, 115, 116, 121
sanction(s), 61, 64
Sankara, 109, 120, 121
Santayana, George, 100
Sasaki, Ken-ichi, 121
scale model, 24
schem(a)(e)(s), 8, 33, 58, 59, 61, 63
  conceptual s., 42, 55, 57, 60, 62–66, 68, 69, 73, 74
  alternative s., 65, 66
  s. vs. content duality, 57, 62, 64
  home s., 67
  s. map, 97
  multiple s., 68
  three-tiered s., 43

scheme concept. 63. *See also* conceptual scheme
Schjeldahl, Peter, 17
scientific heritage, 62
seekers, 105, 108
sel(f)(ves), 1, 29, 41, 45, 82, 86, 98–100, 105–120
  autonomous s., 105
  s.-consciousness, 8, 97
  s.-control, 98
  ego-self, 86
  conventional s., 109, 112, 118, 120
  s.-cultivation, 2
  s.-deception, 105
  s.-definition, 8
  s.-development, 101
  s.-exploration, 9
  s.-fashioning, 9
  s.-identity, 104
  intending s., 107
  s.-interest, 9
  s.-narration, 104
  narratizing s., 104
  newly constituted s., 106
  s.-other duality, 109
  s.-portrait(ure)(s), 8–10
  s.-portrayal(s), 9
  projected s., 104
  s.-realization, 2, 37, 98, 101, 105, 107–110, 117
  s.-recognition, 117, 118
  s.-reference, 110
  s.-scrutiny, 9
  selfishness, 93
  substantive s., 103, 104
  s.-sufficiency, 99
  s.-transformation(s), 2, 97–101, 103, 105, 107, 109–111, 113–115, 117, 119, 121
  uninterpreted s., 91
  unrealized s., 104
Self-Portraits (Rembrandt), 1, 8–10, 14
selection, 1, 32, 46
sens(ation)(es), 62, 63, 119
sense (product of elucidation), 2, 10, 23,
    29, 41, 42, 44, 52, 61, 64–66, 91, 92, 94, 101, 105, 108, 116
sense data, 62, 63
sensory channels, 1
sensory promptings, 62
sentence(s), 58, 63, 76, 77, 79
Shakespeare, William, 71
  Hamlet, 71, 73
shame, 61, 63, 64, 66–68
  Japanese s. culture, 61
show(s), art, 53
  halftime s., 17
Shulamith (Keifer), 8
"Sieg Heil," 8
significance, 1, 36, 41, 45, 52, 53, 89
  moral s., 107
sin, 61, 64
singularis(m)(ts), 13, 15, 19, 21, 22, 45, 75, 75. *See also* critical monism
  s. condition(s), 7, 8, 11, 12, 15, 16, 20, 21, 23, 26, 28, 35, 37, 75; *see also* condition(s)
  meta-s., 21
  s. vs. multiplism, 7–11 *passim*, 23–33 *passim*, 35–39 *passim*
  perpetual s., 21
  super-s., 22
  s. thesis, 23
  universal s., 18
situations, 30, 31, 33, 85, 87, 88, 91–94, 98
  evoking framed s., 86
  interpreted-s., 86
  praxial s., 78
  problem s., 41
  Tibetan s., 85, 86
skeptic(ism)(s), 58, 59
something, 1–3, 17, 24, 41, 44, 45, 49, 51–53, 58, 62, 63, 74, 75, 78, 85, 90, 93, 103, 111, 115–119
soteriolog(ies)(y), 3, 90, 93, 107, 109–111, 113, 120
  s. paradox, 109
  Vedantic s., 103, 111, 112
soteriological predilections, 90

soul, 75, 103, 109
  individual vs. universal s., 108
sounds, 38, 42
Sozanski, Edward, 16, 17
space, 20, 24, 28, 92, 98
  absolute s., 113
  cavernous s., 8
  conversational s., 66
  dialogical s., 38, 39, 114
  inner s., 92, 97
  intimate s., 88
  logical s., 74
  narrative s., 104
  neutral s., 119
  public s., 104
  s. of Supreme Self, 120
speaker(s), 42, 60, 63
  bilingual s., 66, 68
spectacle, 17, 18
specular view, 78
speech, 1
squirrel, 99
stagnation, 99
standard(s), 58, 101
  absolute s., 59
  imperial s., 33
  non-relative s., 61
  overarching s., 32, 59
  s. of precision, 24
  univocal commensurating s., 59
state of affairs, 31, 108
state(s), 53, 54, 61, 100, 105, 108, 112
  analyzable s., 74
  emotional s., 86
  inner s., 9
  realized s., 113, 115, 118
  unattenuated s., 117
  s. of union, 20
Steinberg, Leo, 19, 20
Stevens, Mark, 17
sill life, 99
stor(ies)(y), 29, 36, 41, 72, 90, 91, 104–107
  admissible s., 30
  amusing s., 99
  counterstories, 106

falsifying s., 115, 116
  private s., 42
  untold s., 90
structure(s), 4, 77, 82, 99
  s. as artwork, 51
  determinate s., 79
  linguistic s., 27
  micros., 27, 28, 80
  molecular s., 80
  praxial s., 78
  subvisible s., 52
studio, 92, 97, 99
stuff, 26, 27, 52, 76
  da s. (pre-praxial), 73
suffering, 2, 3, 108, 115
suit, civil, 31
super frame, 22
super level, 22
supplementation, 46
suprahistorical position, 33
Supreme Self, 1, 105, 107–110, 112–
    115, 117, 118, 120, 121
  Vedantic S. S., 103
surmisal, 112
symbiosis, 1, 4
symbol systems, 57, 74
symmetry of cancellations, 20

tad, 108, 109
Tao-painting, 100
taxonomic achievement, 74
term(s), 2, 8, 10, 11, 14, 26–29, 39, 41,
    42, 49, 50, 53, 41, 42, 49, 50,
    53, 63, 64, 77, 90–92, 99, 100,
    103, 105, 111, 112, 120
  bivalent t., 13
  equivalent t., 67
  formal t., 58
  linguistic t., 67
  t. of operative frame, 106, 110
  pragmatic t., 22
  propositional t., 79
  relational t., 14
  schematic t., 43
  symbolic t., 45

tertium non datur, 13
theor(ies)(ists)(y), 33, 52, 72, 111
    conjectural t., 97
    false t., 59
    incompatible t., 54
    t. of interpretation, 7, 71
    rival t., 111
theoretical diagnosis, 33
thing(s), 26, 42, 45, 52, 53, 63, 71, 72,
       74, 101, 112, 119
    common t., 26
    lengths of t., 77
    middle-sized t., 80, 81
    nature of t., 63, 80, 110, 121
    real t., 43
    same vs. different t., 2, 16, 18, 25, 27,
       28, 38, 39, 81, 116, 121
    silly t., 92
    single t., 7, 80, 81
    third t., 14
thirst-quenchingness, 81
Thom, Paul, 2–4, 41, 43, 71, 108
"Thou Art That," 1, 105, 108, 110, 114,
      115, 118, 119
thought, 46, 57, 66, 75, 82, 109
    Enlightenment t., 19
    Indian t., 110
    rational t., 119
    state of no-t., 100
Tibetan Buddhist community, 86
time, 14, 15, 89, 104
tolerance, 12, 13
    interpretive t., 11
tongue, 61, 100
    European t., 61
touch, 17
    unmediated t., 63
touchstones, 112
trace, 100
Tractatus (Wittgenstein), 110
tradition(s), 38, 39, 42, 57, 101, 121
    aestheticist t., 18, 27
    Hindu t., 39
    religious t., 116
    Vedantic t., 117, 120

transformation, 2, 45–47, 110, 113,
      117, 120
    self-t., 2, 97–100, 105, 110, 114
    work-t., 46
transition, 106, 107
translatability, 24, 60, 65–69
translation method, 54
translation(s), 39, 46, 60, 65–68
treasure(s), 59
tribunal, 62
tronies, 9, 10
truth, 4, 13, 26, 50, 57, 76, 78, 82, 108, 119
    absolute t., 59, 120
    t.-claims, 91
    conventional t., 120
    t.-determination, 78
    dualistic t., 120
    objective t., 63
    relative t., 58, 59, 68
    t.-values, 13, 58
Truth, the, 109

unattenuated state, 117
understandability, 66, 68, 69
understanding, 2, 3, 12, 13, 28, 30, 36,
      38, 61, 6–69, 71, 86, 101, 119
    cultural u., 42
    mutual u., 59
    non-u., 38
uninterpretability, 103
union, 20
unity, 7, 100
    temporal u., 104
    undifferentiated u., 116
unsustainability, 105
Upanisads, 39
Ur-text, 46
utterance(s), 4, 65, 117

valid(ation)(ity), 103, 121
    invalidity, 110
    universal v., 116
value, 41, 101
    bipolar v., 58
    v. claims, 57, 60

value (*continued*)
  soteriological v., 101
  supreme v., 80
  transformational v., 120
values, 91, 104, 105
  bivalent v., 13
  multivalent v., 13
  truth-v., 13, 58
Van De Wetering, Ernst , 8–10
Van Gogh, Vincent, 1, 7, 8, 11, 71
  The Potato Eaters, 1, 7
vantage point, 66
Varanasi(ans), 16
Vedanta, 39
Vedantic orientation, 109
Vedantic rationale, 37
Vedantic tradition, 117
Vedas, 39
vehicles, 85, 97
  transformative v., 109, 110, 117, 120
verbs, 1, 61
verdicts, 18, 62
  singularist v., 30, 31
Vesuvius, Mount, 92, 98
view(er)(s), 7, 8, 20, 36, 42, 44, 53, 54,
    57, 58, 60, 62, 71, 79, 85, 93–95
  v. of aim of life, 107
  artist's v., 10
  Buddhist v., 93, 94
  contending v., 36
  contrasting v., 103
  God's eye point of v., 22
  interpreter's v., 4
  narratist v., 103–107
  other's v., 38
  praxial v., 27
  v. of progress, 59
  projectionist v., 50
  relationist v., 52
    r. vs. multiplist v., 59
  religious v., 111

v. of self, 107
specimen v., 103
specular v., 78
Supreme Self v., 103
unorthodox v., 114
Vedantic v., 37
v. of the universe, 54
world v., 57, 62
virtue, 67
vision, paranoiac, 99
Vivekananda, Swami, 109, 115

warrant, 32
  degree of w., 33
weeds, 12
Weisstein, Eric, 14
Weston, Nancy, 30–33
Whorf, Benjamin Lee, 61, 64
will, weakness of, 33
Wittgenstein, Ludwig, 110, 111
  Tractatus, 110
Wong, David, 67
world, 1, 28, 42, 45, 54, 62, 63, 72–75,
    77, 79, 81, 82, 93, 97, 108, 119
  extralinguistic w., 79
  indeterminate w., 75
  knowable w., 78
  w. of objects, 99, 100
  praxial w., 29, 76, 79, 82
  preconceptual w., 78, 79
  prelinguistic w., 77, 78
  real w., 58, 77
  shared w., 111
  undifferentiated, uncountable w., 26,
    27, 80
  unsuspecting w., 61
World, 19, 76
World Series, 17
World Trade Center, New York City, 72
writing(s), 1, 87, 98

VIBS

The **Value Inquiry Book Series** is co-sponsored by:

Titles Published

1. Noel Balzer, *The Human Being as a Logical Thinker*

2. Archie J. Bahm, *Axiology: The Science of Values*

3. H. P. P. (Hennie) Lötter, *Justice for an Unjust Society*

4. H. G. Callaway, *Context for Meaning and Analysis: A Critical Study in the Philosophy of Language*

5. Benjamin S. Llamzon, *A Humane Case for Moral Intuition*

6. James R. Watson, *Between Auschwitz and Tradition: Postmodern Reflections on the Task of Thinking.* A volume in **Holocaust and Genocide Studies**

7. Robert S. Hartman, *Freedom to Live: The Robert Hartman Story*, Edited by Arthur R. Ellis. A volume in **Hartman Institute Axiology Studies**

8. Archie J. Bahm, *Ethics: The Science of Oughtness*

9. George David Miller, *An Idiosyncratic Ethics; Or, the Lauramachean Ethics*

10. Joseph P. DeMarco, *A Coherence Theory in Ethics*

11. Frank G. Forrest, *Valuemetrics*: The Science of Personal and Professional Ethics.* A volume in **Hartman Institute Axiology Studies**

12. William Gerber, *The Meaning of Life: Insights of the World's Great Thinkers*

13. Richard T. Hull, Editor, *A Quarter Century of Value Inquiry: Presidential Addresses of the American Society for Value Inquiry.* A volume in **Histories and Addresses of Philosophical Societies**

14. William Gerber, *Nuggets of Wisdom from Great Jewish Thinkers: From Biblical Times to the Present*

15.   Sidney Axinn, *The Logic of Hope: Extensions of Kant's View of Religion*

16.   Messay Kebede, *Meaning and Development*

17.   Amihud Gilead, *The Platonic Odyssey: A Philosophical-Literary Inquiry into the Phaedo*

18.   Necip Fikri Alican, *Mill's Principle of Utility: A Defense of John Stuart Mill's Notorious Proof.* A volume in **Universal Justice**

19.   Michael H. Mitias, Editor, *Philosophy and Architecture.*

20.   Roger T. Simonds, *Rational Individualism: The Perennial Philosophy of Legal Interpretation.* A volume in **Natural Law Studies**

21.   William Pencak, The Conflict of Law and Justice in the Icelandic Sagas

22.   Samuel M. Natale and Brian M. Rothschild, Editors, *Values, Work, Education: The Meanings of Work*

23.   N. Georgopoulos and Michael Heim, Editors, *Being Human in the Ultimate: Studies in the Thought of John M. Anderson*

24.   Robert Wesson and Patricia A. Williams, Editors, *Evolution and Human Values*

25.   Wim J. van der Steen, *Facts, Values, and Methodology: A New Approach to Ethics*

26.   Avi Sagi and Daniel Statman, *Religion and Morality*

27.   Albert William Levi, *The High Road of Humanity: The Seven Ethical Ages of Western Man*, Edited by Donald Phillip Verene and Molly Black Verene

28.   Samuel M. Natale and Brian M. Rothschild, Editors, *Work Values: Education, Organization, and Religious Concerns*

29.   Laurence F. Bove and Laura Duhan Kaplan, Editors, *From the Eye of the Storm: Regional Conflicts and the Philosophy of Peace.* A volume in **Philosophy of Peace**

30.   Robin Attfield, *Value, Obligation, and Meta-Ethics*

31.   William Gerber, *The Deepest Questions You Can Ask About God: As Answered by the World's Great Thinkers*

32.   Daniel Statman, *Moral Dilemmas*

33.   Rem B. Edwards, Editor, *Formal Axiology and Its Critics*. A volume in **Hartman Institute Axiology Studies**

34.   George David Miller and Conrad P. Pritscher, *On Education and Values: In Praise of Pariahs and Nomads*. A volume in **Philosophy of Education**

35.   Paul S. Penner, *Altruistic Behavior: An Inquiry into Motivation*

36.   Corbin Fowler, *Morality for Moderns*

37.   Giambattista Vico, *The Art of Rhetoric* (*Institutiones Oratoriae*, 1711–1741), from the definitive Latin text and notes, Italian commentary and introduction byGiuliano Crifò.Translated and Edited by Giorgio A. Pinton and Arthur W. Shippee. A volume in **Values in Italian Philosophy**

38.   W. H. Werkmeister, *Martin Heidegger on the Way*. Edited by Richard T. Hull. A volume in **Werkmeister Studies**

39.   Phillip Stambovsky, *Myth and the Limits of Reason*

40.   Samantha Brennan, Tracy Isaacs, and Michael Milde, Editors, *A Question of Values: New Canadian Perspectives in Ethics and Political Philosophy*

41.   Peter A. Redpath, *Cartesian Nightmare: An Introduction to Transcendental Sophistry*. A volume in **Studies in the History of Western Philosophy**

42.   Clark Butler, *History as the Story of Freedom: Philosophy in InterculturalContext*, with responses by sixteen scholars

43.   Dennis Rohatyn, *Philosophy History Sophistry*

44.   Leon Shaskolsky Sheleff, *Social Cohesion and Legal Coercion: A Critique of Weber, Durkheim, and Marx*. Afterword by Virginia Black

45.   Alan Soble, Editor, *Sex, Love, and Friendship: Studies of the Society for the Philosophy of Sex and Love, 1977–1992*. A volume in **Histories and Addresses of Philosophical Societies**

46.   Peter A. Redpath, *Wisdom's Odyssey: From Philosophy to Transcendental Sophistry*. A volume in **Studies in the History of Western Philosophy**

47.   Albert A. Anderson, *Universal Justice: A Dialectical Approach*. A volume in **Universal Justice**

48.   Pio Colonnello, *The Philosophy of José Gaos*. Translated from Italian by Peter Cocozzella. Edited by Myra Moss. Introduction by Giovanni Gullace. A volume in **Values in Italian Philosophy**

49.   Laura Duhan Kaplan and Laurence F. Bove, Editors, *Philosophical Perspectives on Power and Domination: Theories and Practices*. A volume in **Philosophy of Peace**

50.   Gregory F. Mellema, *Collective Responsibility*

51.   Josef Seifert, *What Is Life? The Originality, Irreducibility, and Value of Life*. A volume in **Central-European Value Studies**

52.   William Gerber, *Anatomy of What We Value Most*

53.   Armando Molina, *Our Ways: Values and Character*, Edited by Rem B. Edwards. A volume in **Hartman Institute Axiology Studies**

54.   Kathleen J. Wininger, *Nietzsche's Reclamation of Philosophy*. A volume in **Central-European Value Studies**

55.   Thomas Magnell, Editor, *Explorations of Value*

56.   HPP (Hennie) Lötter, *Injustice, Violence, and Peace: The Case of South Africa*. A volume in **Philosophy of Peace**

57.   Lennart Nordenfelt, *Talking About Health: A Philosophical Dialogue*. A volume in **Nordic Value Studies**

58.   Jon Mills and Janusz A. Polanowski, *The Ontology of Prejudice*. A volume in **Philosophy and Psychology**

59.   Leena Vilkka, *The Intrinsic Value of Nature*

60.   Palmer Talbutt, Jr., Rough Dialectics: *Sorokin's Philosophy of Value*, with contributions by Lawrence T. Nichols and Pitirim A. Sorokin

61.   C. L. Sheng, *A Utilitarian General Theory of Value*

62.   George David Miller, *Negotiating Toward Truth: The Extinction of Teachers and Students*. Epilogue by Mark Roelof Eleveld. A volume in **Philosophy of Education**

63.   William Gerber, *Love, Poetry, and Immortality: Luminous Insights of the World's Great Thinkers*

64.   Dane R. Gordon, Editor, *Philosophy in Post-Communist Europe*. A volume in **Post-Communist European Thought**

65.   Dane R. Gordon and Józef Niznik, Editors, *Criticism and Defense of Rationality in Contemporary Philosophy*. A volume in **Post-Communist European Thought**

66.   John R. Shook, *Pragmatism: An Annotated Bibliography, 1898-1940*. With contributions by E. Paul Colella, Lesley Friedman, Frank X. Ryan, and Ignas K. Skrupskelis

67.   Lansana Keita, *The Human Project and the Temptations of Science*

68.   Michael M. Kazanjian, *Phenomenology and Education: Cosmology, Co-Being, and Core Curriculum*. A volume in **Philosophy of Education**

69.   James W. Vice, *The Reopening of the American Mind: On Skepticism and Constitutionalism*

70.   Sarah Bishop Merrill, *Defining Personhood: Toward the Ethics of Quality in Clinical Care*

71.   Dane R. Gordon, *Philosophy and Vision*

72.   Alan Milchman and Alan Rosenberg, Editors, *Postmodernism and the Holocaust*. A volume in **Holocaust and Genocide Studies**

73.   Peter A. Redpath, *Masquerade of the Dream Walkers: Prophetic Theology from the Cartesians to Hegel*. A volume in **Studies in the History of Western Philosophy**

74.   Malcolm D. Evans, *Whitehead and Philosophy of Education: The Seamless Coat of Learning*. A volume in **Philosophy of Education**

75.   Warren E. Steinkraus, *Taking Religious Claims Seriously: A Philosophy of Religion*, Edited by Michael H. Mitias. A volume in **Universal Justice**

76.   Thomas Magnell, Editor, *Values and Education*

77.   Kenneth A. Bryson, *Persons and Immortality*. A volume in **Natural Law Studies**

78.   Steven V. Hicks, *International Law and the Possibility of a Just World Order: An Essay on Hegel's Universalism*. A volume in **Universal Justice**

79.   E. F. Kaelin, *Texts on Texts and Textuality: A Phenomenology of Literary Art*, Edited by Ellen J. Burns

80.   Amihud Gilead, *Saving Possibilities: A Study in Philosophical Psychology*. A volume in Philosophy and Psychology

81.   André Mineau, *The Making of the Holocaust: Ideology and Ethics in the Systems Perspective*. A volume in **Holocaust and Genocide Studies**

82.   Howard P. Kainz, *Politically Incorrect Dialogues: Topics Not Discussed in Polite Circles*

83.   Veikko Launis, Juhani Pietarinen, and Juha Räikkä, Editors, *Genes and Morality: New Essays*. A volume in **Nordic Value Studies**

84.   Steven Schroeder, *The Metaphysics of Cooperation: A Study of F. D. Maurice*

85.   Caroline Joan ("Kay") S. Picart, *Thomas Mann and Friedrich Nietzsche: Eroticism, Death, Music, and Laughter*. A volume in **Central-European Value Studies**

86.   G. John M. Abbarno, Editor, *The Ethics of Homelessness: Philosophical Perspectives*

87.   James Giles, Editor, *French Existentialism: Consciousness, Ethics, and Relations with Others*. A volume in **Nordic Value Studies**

88.   Deane Curtin and Robert Litke, Editors, *Institutional Violence*. A volume in **Philosophy of Peace**

89.　Yuval Lurie, *Cultural Beings: Reading the Philosophers of Genesis*

90.　Sandra A. Wawrytko, Editor, *The Problem of Evil: An Intercultural Exploration.* A volume in **Philosophy and Psychology**

91.　Gary J. Acquaviva, *Values, Violence, and Our Future.* A volume in **Hartman Institute Axiology Studies**

92.　Michael R. Rhodes, *Coercion: A Nonevaluative Approach*

93.　Jacques Kriel, *Matter, Mind, and Medicine: Transforming the Clinical Method*

94.　Haim Gordon, *Dwelling Poetically: Educational Challenges in Heidegger's Thinking on Poetry.* A volume in **Philosophy of Education**

95.　Ludwig Grünberg, *The Mystery of Values: Studies in Axiology*, Edited by Cornelia Grünberg and Laura Grünberg

96.　Gerhold K. Becker, Editor, *The Moral Status of Persons: Perspectives on Bioethics.* A volume in **Studies in Applied Ethics**

97.　Roxanne Claire Farrar, *Sartrean Dialectics: A Method for Critical Discourse on Aesthetic Experience*

98.　Ugo Spirito, *Memoirs of the Twentieth Century.* Translated from Italian and Edited by Anthony G. Costantini. A volume in **Values in Italian Philosophy**

99.　Steven Schroeder, *Between Freedom and Necessity: An Essay on the Place of Value*

100.　Foster N. Walker, *Enjoyment and the Activity of Mind: Dialogues on Whitehead and Education.* A volume in **Philosophy of Education**

101.　Avi Sagi, Kierkegaard, *Religion, and Existence: The Voyage of the Self.* Translated from Hebrew by Batya Stein

102.　Bennie R. Crockett, Jr., Editor, *Addresses of the Mississippi Philosophical Association.* A volume in **Histories and Addresses of Philosophical Societies**

103.   Paul van Dijk, *Anthropology in the Age of Technology: The Philosophical Contribution of Günther Anders*

104.   Giambattista Vico, *Universal Right*. Translated from Latin and edited by Giorgio Pinton and Margaret Diehl. A volume in **Values in Italian Philosophy**

105.   Judith Presler and Sally J. Scholz, Editors, *Peacemaking: Lessons from the Past, Visions for the Future*. A volume in **Philosophy of Peace**

106.   Dennis Bonnette, *Origin of the Human Species*. A volume in **Studies in the History of Western Philosophy**

107.   Phyllis Chiasson, *Peirce's Pragmatism: The Design for Thinking*. A volume in **Studies in Pragmatism and Values**

108.   Dan Stone, Editor, *Theoretical Interpretations of the Holocaust*. A volume in **Holocaust and Genocide Studies**

109.   Raymond Angelo Belliotti, *What Is the Meaning of Human Life?*

110.   Lennart Nordenfelt, *Health, Science, and Ordinary Language*, with Contributions by George Khushf and K. W. M. Fulford

111.   Daryl Koehn, *Local Insights, Global Ethics for Business*. A volume in **Studies in Applied Ethics**

112.   Matti Häyry and Tuija Takala, Editors, *The Future of Value Inquiry*. A volume in **Nordic Value Studies**

113.   Conrad P. Pritscher, *Quantum Learning: Beyond Duality*

114.   Thomas M. Dicken and Rem B. Edwards, *Dialogues on Values and Centers of Value: Old Friends, New Thoughts*. A volume in **Hartman Institute Axiology Studies**

115.   Rem B. Edwards, *What Caused the Big Bang?* A volume in **Philosophy and Religion**

116.   Jon Mills, Editor, *A Pedagogy of Becoming*. A volume in **Philosophy of Education**

117.   Robert T. Radford, *Cicero: A Study in the Origins of Republican Philosophy*. A volume in **Studies in the History of Western Philosophy**

118.   Arleen L. F. Salles and María Julia Bertomeu, Editors, *Bioethics: Latin American Perspectives*. A volume in **Philosophy in Latin America**

119.   Nicola Abbagnano, *The Human Project: The Year 2000*, with an Interview by Guiseppe Grieco. Translated from Italian by Bruno Martini and Nino Langiulli. Edited with an introduction by Nino Langiulli. A volume in **Studies in the History of Western Philosophy**

120.   Daniel M. Haybron, Editor, *Earth's Abominations: Philosophical Studies of Evil*. A volume in **Personalist Studies**

121.   Anna T. Challenger, *Philosophy and Art in Gurdjieff's* Beelzebub*: A Modern Sufi Odyssey*

122.   George David Miller, *Peace, Value, and Wisdom: The Educational Philosophy of Daisaku Ikeda*. A volume in **Daisaku Ikeda Studies**

123.   Haim Gordon and Rivca Gordon, *Sophistry and Twentieth-Century Art*

124.   Thomas O. Buford and Harold H. Oliver, Editors *Personalism Revisited: Its Proponents and Critics*. A volume in **Histories and Addresses of Philosophical Societies**

125.   Avi Sagi, *Albert Camus and the Philosophy of the Absurd*. Translated from Hebrew by Batya Stein

126.   Robert S. Hartman, *The Knowledge of Good: Critique of Axiological Reason*. Expanded translation from the Spanish by Robert S. Hartman. Edited by Arthur R. Ellis and Rem B. Edwards.A volume in **Hartman Institute Axiology Studies**

127.   Alison Bailey and Paula J. Smithka, Editors. *Community*, *Diversity*, *and Difference: Implications for Peace.* A volume in **Philosophy of Peace**

128.   Oscar Vilarroya, *The Dissolution of Mind: A Fable of How Experience Gives Rise to Cognition*. A volume in **Cognitive Science**

129.   Paul Custodio Bube and Jeffery Geller, Editors, *Conversations with Pragmatism: A Multi-Disciplinary Study*. A volume in **Studies in Pragmatism and Values**

130.   Richard Rumana, *Richard Rorty: An Annotated Bibliography of Secondary Literature*. A volume in **Studies in Pragmatism and Values**

131.   Stephen Schneck, Editor, *Max Scheler's Acting Persons: New Perspectives* A volume in **Personalist Studies**

132.   Michael Kazanjian, *Learning Values Lifelong: From Inert Ideas to Wholes.* A volume in **Philosophy of Education**

133.   Rudolph Alexander Kofi Cain, Alain Leroy Locke: *Race, Culture, and the Education of African American Adults*. A volume in **African American Philosophy**

134.   Werner Krieglstein, *Compassion: A New Philosophy of the Other*

135.   Robert N. Fisher, Daniel T. Primozic, Peter A. Day, and Joel A. Thompson, Editors, *Suffering, Death, and Identity*. A volume in **Personalist Studies**

136.   Steven Schroeder, *Touching Philosophy, Sounding Religion, Placing Education*. A volume in **Philosophy of Education**

137.   Guy DeBrock, *Process Pragmatism: Essays on a Quiet Philosophical Revolution*. A volume in **Studies in Pragmatism and Values**

138.   Lennart Nordenfelt and Per-Erik Liss, Editors, *Dimensions of Health and Health Promotion*

139.   Amihud Gilead, *Singularity and Other Possibilities: Panenmentalist Novelties*

140.   Samantha Mei-che Pang, *Nursing Ethics in Modern China: Conflicting Values and Competing Role Requirements*. A volume in **Studies in Applied Ethics**

141.   Christine M. Koggel, Allannah Furlong, and Charles Levin, Editors, *Confidential Relationships: Psychoanalytic, Ethical, and Legal Contexts*. A volume in **Philosophy and Psychology**

142.   Peter A. Redpath, Editor, *A Thomistic Tapestry: Essays in Memory of Étienne Gilson*. A volume in **Gilson Studies**

143. Deane-Peter Baker and Patrick Maxwell, Editors, *Explorations in Contemporary Continental Philosophy of Religion*. A volume in **Philosophy and Religion**

144. Matti Häyry and Tuija Takala, Editors, *Scratching the Surface of Bioethics*. A volume in **Values in Bioethics**

145. Leonidas Donskis, *Forms of Hatred: The Troubled Imagination in Modern Philosophy and Literature*

146. Andreea Deciu Ritivoi, Editor, *Interpretation and Its Objects: Studies in the Philosophy of Michael Krausz*

147. Herman Stark, *A Fierce Little Tragedy: Thought, Passion, and Self-Formation in the Philosophy Classroom*. A volume in **Philosophy of Education**

148. William Gay and Tatiana Alekseeva, Editors, *Democracy and the Quest for Justice: Russian and American Perspectives*. A volume in **Contemporary Russian Philosophy**

149. Xunwu Chen, *Being and Authenticity*

150. Hugh P. McDonald, *Radical Axiology: A First Philosophy of Values*

151. Dane R. Gordon and David C. Durst, Editors, *Civil Society in Southeast Europe*. A volume in **Post-Communist European Thought**

152. John Ryder and Emil Višňovský, Editors, *Pragmatism and Values: The Central European Pragmatist Forum, Volume One*. A volume in **Studies in Pragmatism and Values**

153. Messay Kebede, *Africa's Quest for a Philosophy of Decolonization*

154. Steven M. Rosen, *Dimensions of Apeiron: A Topological Phenomenology of Space, Time, and Individuation*. A volume in **Philosophy and Psychology**

155. Albert A. Anderson, Steven V. Hicks, and Lech Witkowski, Editors, *Mythos and Logos: How to Regain the Love of Wisdom*. A volume in **Universal Justice**

156. John Ryder and Krystyna Wilkoszewska, Editors, *Deconstruction and Reconstruction: The Central European Pragmatist Forum, Volume Two*. A volume in **Studies in Pragmatism and Values**

157.   Javier Muguerza, *Ethics and Perplexity: Toward a Critique of Dialogical Reason*. Translated from the Spanish by Jody L. Doran. Edited by John R. Welch. A volume in **Philosophy in Spain**

158.   Gregory F. Mellema, *The Expectations of Morality*

159.   Robert Ginsberg, *The Aesthetics of Ruins*

160.   Stan van Hooft, *Life, Death, and Subjectivity: Moral Sources in Bioethics* A volume in **Values in Bioethics**

161.   André Mineau, *Operation Barbarossa: Ideology and Ethics Against Human Dignity*

162.   Arthur Efron, *Expriencing Tess of the D'Urbervilles: A Deweyan Account.* A volume in **Studies in Pragmatism and Values**

163.   Reyes Mate, *Memory of the West: The Contemporaneity of Forgotten Jewish Thinkers.* Translated from the Spanish by Anne Day Dewey. Edited by John R. Welch. A volume in **Philosophy in Spain**

164.   Nancy Nyquist Potter, Editor, *Putting Peace into Practice: Evaluating Policy on Local and Global Levels.* A volume in **Philosophy of Peace**

165.   Matti Häyry, Tuija Takala, and Peter Herissone-Kelly, Editors, *Bioethics and Social Reality.* A volume in **Values in Bioethics**

166.   Maureen Sie, *Justifying Blame: Why Free Will Matters and Why it Does Not.* A volume in **Studies in Applied Ethics**

167.   Leszek Koczanowicz and Beth J. Singer, Editors, *Democracy and the Post-Totalitarian Experience.* A volume in **Studies in Pragmatism and Values**

168.   Michael W. Riley, *Plato's* Cratylus: *Argument, Form, and Structure.* A volume in **Studies in the History of Western Philosophy**

169.   Leon Pomeroy, *The New Science of Axiological Psychology.* Edited by Rem B. Edwards. A volume in **Hartman Institute Axiology Studies**

170.   Eric Wolf Fried, *Inwardness and Morality*

171.   Sami Pihlstrom, *Pragmatic Moral Realism: A Transcendental Defense.* A volume in Studies in **Pragmatism and Values**

172.   Charles C. Hinkley II, *Moral Conflicts of Organ Retrieval: A Case for Constructive Pluralism.* A volume in **Values in Bioethics**

173.   Gábor Forrai and George Kampis, Editors, *Intentionality: Past and Future.* A volume in **Cognitive Science**

174.   Dixie Lee Harris, *Encounters in My Travels: Thoughts Along the Way.* A volume in **Lived Values:Valued Lives**

175.   Lynda Burns, Editor, *Feminist Alliances.* A volume in **Philosophy and Women**

176.   George Allan and Malcolm D. Evans, *A Different Three Rs for Education.* A volume in **Philosophy of Education**

177.   Robert A. Delfino, Editor, *What are We to Understand Gracia to Mean?: Realist Challenges to Metaphysical Neutralism.* A volume in **Gilson Studies**

178.   Constantin V. Ponomareff and Kenneth A. Bryson, *The Curve of the Sacred: An Exploration of Human Spirituality.* A volume in **Philosophy and Religion**

179.   John Ryder, Gert Rüdiger Wegmarshaus, Editors, *Education for a Democratic Society: Central European Pragmatist Forum, Volume Three.* A volume in **Studies in Pragmatism and Values**

180.   Florencia Luna, *Bioethics and Vulnerability: A Latin American View.* A volume in **Values in Bioethics**

181.   John Kultgen and Mary Lenzi, Editors, *Problems for Democracy.* A volume in **Philosophy of Peace**

182.   David Boersema and Katy Gray Brown, Editors, *Spiritual and Political Dimensions of Nonviolence and Peace.* A volume in **Philosophy of Peace**

183.   Daniel P. Thero, *Understanding Moral Weakness.* A volume in **Studies in the History of Western Philosophy**

184.   Scott Gelfand and John R. Shook, Editors, *Ectogenesis: Artificial Womb Technology and the Future of Human Reproduction.* A volume in **Values in Bioethics**

185.   Piotr Jaroszyński, *Science in Culture*. A volume in **Gilson Studies**

186.   Matti Häyry, Tuija Takala, Peter Herissone-Kelly, Editors, *Ethics in Biomedical Research: International Perspectives*. A volume in **Values in Bioethics**

187.   Michael Krausz, *Interpretation and Transformation: Explorations in Art and the Self*. A volume in **Interpretation and Translation**